VBScript Language
Pocket Reference

*Steven Roman, Ron Petrusha,
and Paul Lomax*

O'REILLY®

Beijing · Cambridge · Farnham · Köln · Paris · Sebastopol · Taipei · Tokyo

VB.NET Language Pocket Reference
by Steven Roman, Ron Petrusha, and Paul Lomax

Copyright © 2003 O'Reilly & Associates, Inc. All rights reserved.
Printed in the United States of America.

Published by O'Reilly & Associates, Inc., 1005 Gravenstein Highway North,
Sebastopol, CA 95472.

O'Reilly & Associates books may be purchased for educational,
business, or sales promotional use. Online editions are also available
for most titles (*safari.oreilly.com*). For more information, contact our
corporate/institutional sales department: (800) 998-9938 or
corporate@oreilly.com.

Editor:	Ron Petrusha
Production Editor:	Sarah Sherman
Cover Designer:	Emma Colby
Interior Designer:	David Futato

Printing History:

November 2002:	First Edition

0-596-00428-1
[C]

Contents

Visual Basic .NET Language Pocket Reference

Introduction

Visual Basic .NET is a radically new version of Microsoft Visual Basic, the world's most widely used rapid application development (RAD) package. Visual Basic .NET is designed to work directly with Microsoft's .NET platform, which includes a Framework Class Library to facilitate application development, a Common Language Runtime to provide a managed execution environment, and a Common Type System to insure interoperability among all languages that support the .NET platform.

The *Visual Basic .NET Language Pocket Reference* is a quick reference guide to Visual Basic 7.0, the first version of Visual Basic .NET. It contains a concise description of all language elements by category. These include language elements implemented by the Visual Basic compiler, as well as all procedures and functions implemented in the Microsoft.VisualBasic namespace. It does not attempt to document the core classes of the .NET Framework Class Library.

The purpose of this quick reference is to aid readers who need to look up some basic detail of Visual Basic syntax or usage. It is not intended to be a tutorial or user guide; at least a basic familiarity with Visual Basic is assumed.

Font Conventions

Constant Width
> Used to indicate code examples, types and type members, statements, constants, and keywords.

Constant Width Italic
> Used to indicate replaceable parameters.

Italic
> Used to indicate new terms, filenames, URLs, and email addresses.

Visual Basic Conventions

The "rules" for Visual Basic (VB) code are very simple:

- VB is a case-insensitive programming language; that is, the compiler ignores case when reading VB code. So myVar, MyVar, MYvar, and MYVAR all refer to the same variable. Note that Visual Studio imposes a uniform casing on all language elements, although this is not a requirement of the compiler.

- White space (except for line breaks) is ignored when reading VB code.

- Line breaks mark the end of a complete statement; complete VB statements must occupy a single line.

- If you want to break a single statement over several lines, you can use the line continuation character, an underscore (_), which must be preceded by a space and must be the last character on the line that is to be continued.

- If you want to combine multiple statements on a single line, you can use the colon (:). Among other uses, it is commonly used to imitate C++ and C# syntax for inheritance. For example, the code fragment:

```
Public Class MainForm
    Inherits Form
```

can be shortened as follows:

```
Public Class MainForm : Inherits Form
```

• Two comment symbols are used: the apostrophe (') and the Rem keyword. They may appear at any place within a line.

Data Types

Whether VB is a weakly or a semi-strongly typed language depends on the Option Explicit setting. (The statement must appear at the top of a code module.) If Off, VB is a weakly typed language; variables need not be declared in advance, and all undeclared variables will be cast as type Object until they are initialized. If On (its default setting), each variable must be declared in advance, but its data type need not be specified. If no type is explicitly declared, variables are cast as type Object until their first use.

Although VB recognizes a number of "intrinsic" data types, each is really a wrapper around a data type found in the .NET Common Type System (CTS). VB recognizes the following intrinsic types:

Boolean
> A logical (True or False) value. Corresponds to System.Boolean.

Byte
> A signed 8-bit numeric data type. Corresponds to System.Byte.

Char
> A 16-bit character data type (character code). Corresponds to System.Char.

Date
> A date or time value. Corresponds to System.DataTime.

Decimal

A decimal or currency value. Corresponds to System.Decimal.

Double

A double-precision floating point value. Corresponds to System.Double.

Integer

A signed 32-bit integral data type. Corresponds to System.Int32.

Long

A signed 64-bit integral data type. Corresponds to System.Int64.

Object

A reference to an object. Object is VB's "universal" data type and corresponds to System.Object.

Short

A signed 16-bit integral data type. Corresponds to System.Int16.

Single

A single-precision floating point value. Corresponds to System.Single.

String

A reference type pointing to a fixed-length character string. Corresponds to System.String.

A number of other data types are available from the .NET CTS but are not wrapped by a corresponding VB intrinsic data type. These include:

System.SByte

A signed 8-bit integral data type.

System.UInt16

An unsigned 16-bit integral data type.

System.UInt32

An unsigned 32-bit integral data type.

System.UInt64

An unsigned 64-bit integral data type.

VB also allows you to create user-defined reference types by using the `Class...End Class` construct and user-defined value types by using the `Structure...End Structure` construct.

Any of these data types can be used as a member of an array. Arrays can have a single dimension, or they can be multidimensional (up to 60 dimensions). The first element in an array is always at position 0.

Variables

VB does not require that variables be declared before they are used unless `Option Explicit` is `On` (its default value). In that case, you can declare variables using the `Dim`, `Public`, `Private`, `Protected`, `Friend`, or `Protected Friend` statements.

A variable name in VB must satisfy the following requirements:

- It must be 16,383 or fewer characters in length.
- It must begin with an alphabetic character or an underscore.
- It cannot include embedded spaces.
- It cannot contain any special (i.e., non-alphabetic, non-numeric) character other than an underscore.
- It must be unique within its scope.

Operators and Precedence

VB supports the following operators:

Operator	Description
+	Addition, string concatenation
+=	Increment and assign
-	Subtraction, unary operator
-=	Subtract and assign
/	Division
/=	Divide and assign
\	Integer division (no remainder)
\=	Integer division and assignment
Mod	Modulo arithmetic
*	Multiplication
*=	Multiply and assign
^	Exponentiation
^=	Exponentiation and assignment
&	String concatenation
&=	String concatenation and assignment
=	Equality, assignment
Is	Equality (for object references)
<	Less than
<=, =<	Less than or equal to
>	Greater than
>=, =>	Greater than or equal to
<>, ><	Not equal to
And	Logical or bitwise conjunction
AndAlso	Logical conjunction with short-circuiting
Or	Logical or bitwise disjunction
OrElse	Logical disjunction with short-circuiting

Operator	Description
Not	Logical or bitwise negation
Xor	Logical or bitwise exclusion

Expressions are evaluated in the following order:

1. Arithmetic operators
    a. Exponentiation
    b. Division and multiplication
    c. Integer division
    d. Modulo arithmetic
    e. Addition and subtraction
2. Concatenation operators
3. Logical operators
    a. Not
    b. And, AndAlso
    c. Or, OrElse
    d. X

If two or more operators in an expression have the same order of precedence, they are evaluated from left to right.

Constants

VB recognizes the following intrinsic constants:

Call Type Constants

vbGet   vbMethod
vbLet   vbSet

Comparison Constants

vbBinaryCompare   vbTextCompare

Date and Time Constants

vbSunday
vbMonday
vbTuesday
vbWednesday
vbThursday
vbFriday

vbSaturday
vbUseSystem
vbUseSystemDayOfWeek
vbFirstJan1
vbFirstFourDays
vbFirstFullWeek

Date Format Constants

vbGeneralDate
vbLongDate
vbLongTime

vbShortDate
vbShortTime

Error Constant

vbObjectError

File Attributes

vbArchive
vbDirectory
vbHidden
vbReadOnly

vbNormal
vbSystem
vbVolume

Logical and Tristate Constants

False
True
vbFalse

vbTrue
vbUseDefault

Message Box Constants

Buttons constants

vbAbortRetryIgnore
vbMsgBoxHelp
vbOKCancel
vbOKOnly

vbRetryCancel
vbYesNo
vbYesNoCancel

Default button constants

vbDefaultButton1   vbDefaultButton3
vbDefaultButton2

Icon constants

vbCritical   vbInformation
vbExclamation   vbQuestion

Modality constants

vbApplicationModal   vbSystemModal

Return value constants

vbAbort   vbOK
vbCancel   vbRetry
vbIgnore   vbYes
vbNo

Miscellaneous constants

vbMsgBoxRight   vbMsgBoxSetForeground
vbMsgBoxRtlReading

Special Character Constants

vbBack   vbNewLine
vbCr   vbNullChar
vbCrLf   vbNullString
vbFormFeed   vbTab
vbLf   vbVerticalTab

Variable Subtype Constants

vbArray   vbInteger
vbBoolean   vbLong
vbByte   vbNull
vbCurrency   vbObject
vbDate   vbSingle
vbDecimal   vbString

vbDouble	vbUserDefinedType
vbEmpty	vbVariant

Window Style Constants

vbHide	vbNarrow
vbHiragana	vbNormalFocus
vbKatakana	vbNormalNoFocus
vbLinguisticCasing	vbProperCase
vbLowerCase	vbSimplifiedChinese
vbMaximizedFocus	vbTraditionalChinese
vbMinimizedFocus	vbUpperCase
vbMinimizedNoFocus	vbWide

User-defined constants can be declared using the Const statement.

Enumerations

The Microsoft.VisualBasic namespace also defines a number of enumerations. Many of their members are functionally identical to almost identically named constants listed in the aforementioned "Constants" section.

AppWinStyle Enumeration

Determines the appearance and behavior of the window opened by the *Shell* function.

Hide	MinimizedNoFocus
MaximizedFocus	NormalFocus
MinimizedFocus	NormalNoFocus

CallType Enumeration

Defines the type of procedure invoked by the *CallByName* function.

Get	Set
Method	

CompareMethod Enumeration

Used with a variety of string comparison methods (such as *InStr*, *StrComp*, and *Replace*) to determine whether the comparison is case sensitive or insensitive.

Binary	Text

ControlChars Class

Values representing a number of control characters are available as static read-only fields of the ControlChars class. They can be referenced just as enumerated members; for example:

```
Addr = "123 West St. & ControlChars.CrLf & _
       "Apt. 12C"
```

Back	NewLine
Cr	NullChar
CrLf	Quote
FormFeed	Tab
Lf	VerticalTab

DateFormat Enumeration

Defines the format of the date returned by the *FormatDateTime* function.

GeneralDate	ShortDate
LongDate	ShortTime
LongTime	

DateInterval Enumeration

Defines the date interval for date/time functions, such as *DateDiff*, *DatePart*, and *DateAdd*.

Day	Quarter
DayOfYear	Second
Hour	Weekday
Minute	WeekOfYear
Month	Year

DueDate Enumeration

Used with the *FV*, *IPmt*, *NPer*, *Pmt*, *PPmt*, *PV*, and *Rate* functions to define whether a payment is due at the beginning or end of a period.

```
BegOfPeriod              EndOfPeriod
```

FileAttribute Enumeration

Used with the *Dir*, *GetAttr*, and *SetAttr* functions to set a file's attributes or to retrieve files with particular attributes set.

```
Archive                  ReadOnly
Directory                System
Hidden                   Volume
Normal
```

FirstDayOfWeek Enumeration

Used with the *DatePart*, *DateDiff*, *Weekday*, and *WeekdayName* functions to define the first day of the week and to interpret the function's return value.

```
Friday                   System
Monday                   Tuesday
Saturday                 Thursday
Sunday                   Wednesday
```

FirstWeekOfYear Enumeration

Used with the *DatePart* and *DateDiff* functions to define the first week of the year and to interpret the function's return value.

```
FirstFourDays            Jan1
FirstFullWeek            System
```

MsgBoxResult Enumeration

Represents the return value of the *MsgBox* function.

Abort	OK
Cancel	Retry
Ignore	Yes
No	

MsgBoxStyle Enumeration

Defines the appearance and behavior of a message box.

AbortRetryIgnore	MsgBoxRtlREading
ApplicationModal	MsgBoxSetForeground
Critical	OKCancel
DefaultButton1	OKOnly
DefaultButton2	Question
DefaultButton3	RetryCancel
Exclamation	SystemModal
Information	YesNo
MsgBoxHelp	YesNoCancel
MsgBoxRight	

OpenAccess Enumeration

Used with the *FileOpen* function to determine how the file can be accessed.

Default	ReadWrite
Read	Write

OpenMode Enumeration

Used with the *FileOpen* function and returned by the *FileAttr* function and indicates the file access mode. The Microsoft.VisualBasic namespace also defines an OpenModeTypes enumeration that is identical to OpenMode except for adding an Any member.

Append   Output
Binary   Random
Input

OpenShare Enumeration

Used with the *FileOpen* function to determine the file's share level.

Default   LockWrite
LockRead   Shared
LockReadWrite

TriState Enumeration

Used with the *FormatCurrency*, *FormatNumber*, and *FormatPercent* functions to control the format of a number.

False   UseDefault
True

VariantType Enumeration

Returned by the *VarType* function to indicate the data type of a variable.

Array   Error
Boolean   Integer
Byte   Long
Char   Null
Currency   Object
DataObject   Short
Date   Single
Decimal   String
Double   UserDefinedType
Empty   Variant

VbStrConv Enumeration

Supplied as a parameter to the *StrConv* function to indicate how a string is to be converted.

Hiragana	ProperCase
Katakana	SimplifiedChinese
LinguisticCasing	TraditionalChinese
LowerCase	UpperCase
Narrow	Wide
None	

Object Programming

Unlike previous versions of VB, VB.NET is a fully object-oriented programming language. This object orientation has two aspects: access to the .NET Framework Class Library (FCL), and the ability to define and instantiate custom classes using inheritance.

.NET Framework Class Library

The .NET Framework Class Library is an object-oriented library consisting of thousands of system and application types (classes, structures, interfaces, delegates, and enumerations) organized in namespaces. The namespaces and types of the .NET FCL offer a wide range of functionality, from wrappers to classic Win32 API functions to diagnostics and debugging to input/output to data access, Windows forms programming, and web application and web service development. In fact, most of the "intrinsic" functions and procedures that are part of the VB.NET language are implemented as members of classes in the Microsoft.VisualBasic namespace.

In order to access the types in a namespace, the compiler must be provided with a reference to its assembly. This is done with the /r switch using the VB command line compiler. When a type is instantiated or a type member is invoked, ordinarily the type's fully qualified namespace must be included. For example, a new instance of an ApplicationException class is generated by the following code fragment:

```
Dim e As New System.ApplicationException()
```

As an alternative, you can have the compiler or the Visual Studio design-time resolve an unqualified object reference by using the Imports directive to import a type's namespace. The Imports directive appears at the top of a file, after any Option statements and before any type or module definitions. Using Imports, we can instantiate an ApplicationException object as follows:

```
Dim e As New ApplicationException()
```

Custom Types and Classes

In addition to accessing the functionality of the .NET FCL, you can also define your own custom types, including custom classes. In defining a class, you can take advantage of *inheritance*; that is, you can indicate that your class derives from another class, either from a class in the .NET FCL or from another custom class. In this case, your class automatically inherits the functionality of its base class. You can even take advantage of inheritance without explicitly specifying an inherited class. All classes automatically inherit from type System.Object, and all structures (which cannot take advantage of inheritance directly) automatically inherit from type System.ValueType. For instance, consider the following code:

```
Public Class AppClass
Public Shared Sub Main
   Dim obj As New AppClass
   System.Console.WriteLine(obj.ToString)
```

```
    End Sub
End Class
```

When compiled, the code produces the following output:

```
AppClass
```

The code calls the `AppClass.ToString` method. But the `ToString` method isn't explicitly defined; instead, it is inherited from the `Object` class.

Along with inherited members, you can also access any members that you defined in your class. Any particular class member can be either an *instance* member or a *shared* member. Instance members require that an object of the class be instantiated, and that the member (and its value, if there is one) belongs to that instance. Shared members do not require an object instance, and instead can be invoked using the class itself. If a shared member has a value, it is shared across all instances of a class.

VB supports three different kinds of members: fields, properties, and methods. The following section examines each of these.

Fields, Properties, and Methods

A *field* is simply a publicly accessible constant or variable. Because it is usually undesirable to give users of a class unrestricted access to its data, fields typically consist of constants or read-only variables. (Read-only variables are not completely read-only; values can be assigned to them when the variable is declared and initialized, as well as in the class constructor.) For example:

```
Public Class FieldClass
    Public ReadOnly Value As Integer = 100
    Public Const Pi = Math.Pi

    Public Sub New( )
    End Sub
```

```
      Public Sub New(x As Integer)
         Value = x
      End Sub
   End Class
```

A *property* provides a public interface to a class' state information. A property can consist of either a get accessor (which returns the property value), a set accessor (which sets the property value), or both. For example, the following code defines an Age property for the Employee class:

```
   Public Class Employee

      Private EmployeeAge As Integer

      Public Property Age( ) As Integer
         Get
            Return EmployeeAge
         End Get
         Set
            EmployeeAge = Value
         End Set
      End Property
   End Class
```

A *method* represents an action or operation that is performed upon the class. VB recognizes functions, which are declared with the Function...End Function construct, and subroutines, which are declared with the Sub...End Sub construct. Functions return a value to the caller; subroutines do not. Both functions and subroutines can include a list of parameters to be passed to the procedure by the caller. For example:

```
   Public Class MathLib
      Public Sub SwapNumbers(ByRef Num1 As Integer, _
                             ByRef Num2 As Integer)
         Dim Temp As Integer
         Temp = Num2
         Num2 = Num1
         Num1 = Temp
      End Sub
```

```
    Public Function Pi() As Double
        Return System.Math.Pi
    End Function
End Class
```

By default, arguments are passed to functions and subroutines *by value*; that is, the function or subroutine is provided with a copy of the argument, and any changes made to the argument by the function or subroutine are discarded when control returns to the caller. This behavior can be overridden, and an argument can be passed to a function or subroutine *by reference*; that is, the address of the data is provided to the function or subroutine. To pass an argument by reference, precede the parameter in the function or subroutine's parameter list with the ByRef keyword.

You can call a subroutine in either of the following ways:

```
oMath.SwapNumbers(x, y)
Call oMath.SwapNumbers(x, y)
```

You call a function as follows:

```
Result = oMath.Pi()
```

However, if you're not interested in the function's return value, you can also call the function as if it were a subroutine.

Program Structure

When a class or structure is instantiated, its class constructor (which in VB is a subroutine named New) is automatically invoked. In addition, each executable requires an entry point in the form of a function or subroutine named Main. For example:

```
Public Class PgmStruct

    Private Value As Integer

    Public Sub New(x As Integer)
        Value = x
    End Sub
```

```
    Public Shared Sub Main( )
        Dim obj As New PgmStruct(100)
        Console.WriteLine(obj.Value)
    End Sub
End Class
```

Array Handling

Erase Statement

Erase *arraylist*

arraylist   *required; String literal*
    A list of array variables to clear

Description: Releases an array object. This is equivalent to setting the array variable to Nothing. More than one array can be specified by using commas to delimit *arraylist*.

IsArray Function   Microsoft.VisualBasic.Information

IsArray(*varname*)

varname   *required; any variable*
    A variable that may be an array

Return Value: Boolean (True or False)

Description: Tests whether an object variable points to an array. Note that an uninitialized array returns False.

Join Function   Microsoft.VisualBasic.Strings

result = Join(*sourcearray*, [*delimiter*])

sourcearray   *required; String or Object array*
    Array whose elements are to be concatenated

delimiter   *optional; String*
    Character used to delimit the individual values in the string

Return Value: String

Description: Concatenates an array of values into a delimited string using a specified *delimiter*, or, if no *delimiter* is specified, a space.

LBound Function   Microsoft.VisualBasic.Information

LBound(*array*[, *rank*])

array   *required; any array*
    An array whose lower bound is to be determined

rank   *optional; Integer*
    The dimension whose lower bound is desired

Return Value: An Integer whose value is 0

Description: Determines the lower boundary of a specified dimension of an array. The lower boundary is the smallest subscript you can access within the specified array.

ReDim Statement

ReDim [Preserve] *varname*(*subscripts*) _
                [, *varname*(*subscripts*) ...]

Preserve   *optional; Keyword*
    Preserves the data within an array when changing the only or last dimension

varname   *required; String literal*
    Name of the variable

subscripts   *required; Numeric*
    Number of elements and dimensions of the array, using the syntax:

    upper [, *upper*] ...

    The number of upper bounds specified is the number of dimensions. Each upper bound specifies the size of the corresponding coordinate.

Description: Used within a procedure to resize and reallocate storage space for an array

---

UBound Function   Microsoft.VisualBasic.Information

UBound(*array*[, *rank*])

array   *required; Any*
> The name of the array

rank   *optional; Integer*
> A number specifying the dimension of the array; if omitted, its value defaults to 1

Return Value: Integer; returns −1 if the array is uninitialized

Description: Indicates the upper limit of a specified coordinate of an array. The upper boundary is the largest subscript you can use with that coordinate.

VBFixedArray Attribute   Microsoft.VisualBasic.VBFixedArrayAttribute

New(*size1*[, *size2*])

size1   *required; Integer*
> The upper limit of the array's first dimension

size2   *optional; Integer*
> The upper limit of the array's second dimension

Description: Defines a fixed array. It can be used in defining fixed arrays within structures, particularly structures that are to be passed to Win32 API functions.

Collection Objects

Collection.Add Method   Microsoft.VisualBasic.Collection

objectvariable.Add *item* [, *key*, *before*, *after*]

objectvariable   *required; Collection Object*
> The Collection object to which an item is to be added

item   *required; Object*
> An object of any type that specifies the member to add to the collection

---

key   *optional; String*
   A unique string expression that specifies a key string that can
   be used, instead of a positional index, to access a member of
   the collection

before   *optional; Object*
   Index or key of the item after which the new item is to be
   added

after   *optional; Object*
   Index or key of the item before which the new item is to be
   added

Description: Adds an item to a particular position in a collection,
or to the end of the collection if no positioned specified.

Collection.Count Property   Microsoft.VisualBasic.Collection

objectvariable.Count

objectvariable   *required; Collection Object*
   An object variable of type Collection

Description: Returns an Integer containing the number of
members in the collection.

Collection.Item Method   Microsoft.VisualBasic.Collection

objectvariable.Item(*index*)

objectvariable   *required; Collection Object*
   An object variable of type Collection

index   *required; Integer or String*
   The index (the ordinal position) or the unique key name of
   the object in the collection

Description: Returns the member of the collection for the specified key or ordinal position.

Collection.Remove Method   Microsoft.VisualBasic.Collection

objectvariable.Remove(*index*)

objectvariable   *required; Collection Object*
   An object variable of the Collection type

---

index   *required; Integer or String*
> The ordinal position or the unique key name of the item to remove

Description: Removes a member from a collection.

Conditional Compilation

#Const Directive

```
#Const constantname = expression
```

constantname   *required; String literal*
> Name of the constant

expression   *required; literal*
> Any combination of literal values, other conditional compilation constants defined with the #Const directive, and arithmetic or logical operators except Is

Description: Defines a conditional compiler constant.

#If...Then...#Else Directive

```
#If expression Then
    statements
[#ElseIf furtherexpression Then
    [elseifstatements]]
[#Else
    [elsestatements]]
#End If
```

expression   *required*
> An expression made up of literals, operators, and conditional compiler constants that will evaluate to True or False

statements   *required*
> One or more lines of code or compiler directives, which is executed if *expression* evaluates to True

furtherexpression   *optional*
> An expression made up of literals, operators, and conditional compiler constants that will evaluate to True or False.

furtherexpression is only evaluated if the preceding expression evaluates to False

elseifstatements *optional*

One or more lines of code or compiler directives, which is executed if *furtherexpression* evaluates to True

elsestatements *optional*

One or more lines of code or compiler directives, which are executed if *expression* or *furtherexpression* evaluates to False

Description: Defines a block or blocks of code that are only included in the compiled application when a particular condition is met, allowing you to create more than one version of the application using the same source code.

Conditionally including a block of code is a two-step process:

- Use the #Const directive to assign a value to a conditional compiler constant.
- Evaluate the conditional compiler constant using the #If... Then...#End If statement block.

Only code blocks whose expressions evaluate to True are included in the executable. You can use the #Else statement to execute code when the #If...Then expression evaluates to False. You can also use an #ElseIf statement to evaluate more expressions if previous expressions in the same block have evaluated to False.

CBool Function

CBool(*expression*)

expression *required; String or Numeric*

Any numeric expression or a string representation of a numeric value

Named Arguments: No

Return Value: *expression* converted to Boolean data type (True or False)

Description: Casts *expression* as a Boolean data type. When a numeric value is converted to Boolean, any nonzero value is converted to True, and zero is converted to False.

If the expression to be converted is a string, the string must be capable of being evaluated as a number, or it must be "True" or "False". Any other string generates an exception. For example, CBool("one") results in a type mismatch error, whereas CBool("1") is converted to True, and CBool("True") is converted to True.

CByte Function

CByte(*expression*)

expression   *required; String or Numeric*
    A string or numeric expression that evaluates to a number between 0 and 255

Named Arguments: No

Return Value: *expression* converted to Byte data type

Description: Converts *expression* to a Byte data type. If the expression to be converted is a string, the string must be capable of conversion to a numeric expression; this can be checked using the *IsNumeric* function. If *expression* evaluates to less than 0 or more than 255, an exception is generated. If the value of *expression* is not a whole number, *CByte* rounds the number prior to conversion.

CChar Function

CChar(*expression*)

expression   *required; String*
    Any string expression

Named Arguments: No

Return Value: A value of type Char

Description: Converts the first character in a string *expression* to a Char data type.

CDate Function

CDate(*expression*)

expression   *required; String or Numeric*
   Any valid representation of a date and time

Named Arguments: No

Return Value: *expression* converted into a Date data type

Description: Converts *expression* to a Date data type. The format of *expression*—the order of day, month, and year—is determined by the locale setting of the local computer. To be certain a date is recognized correctly by *CDate*, the month, day, and year elements of *expression* must be in the same sequence as the local computer's regional settings; otherwise, the *CDate* function has no idea, for example, that 4 was supposed to be the fourth day of the month, not the month of April. The earliest date that can be handled by the Date data type is 01/01/100. The latest date that can be handled by the Date data type is 12/31/9999.

CDbl Function

CDbl(*expression*)

expression   *required; Numeric or String*
   A number or a string representation of a number

Named Arguments: No

Return Value: *expression* cast as a Double data type

Description: Converts *expression* to a Double data type. If *expression* is not numeric, or if its value is outside the range of the Double data type, an exception is generated.

CDec Function

CDec(*expression*)

expression   *required; Numeric or String*
   A numeric value or a string representation of a number

Named Arguments: No

Return Value: *expression* cast as a Decimal type

Description: Converts *expression* to a Decimal data type. If *expression* is not numeric or is outside the range of the Decimal data type, an exception is generated. Use the *IsNumeric* function to test whether *expression* evaluates to a number.

CInt Function

CInt(*expression*)

expression   *required; Numeric or String*
    A numeric value or a string representation of a number

Named Arguments: No

Return Value: *expression* cast as an Integer

Description: Converts *expression* to an Integer data type. If *expression* has a fractional value, it is rounded. When the fractional part of *expression* is exactly .5, *CInt* always rounds it to the nearest even number. If *expression* is not numeric or is outside the range of the Integer data type, an exception is generated. Use *IsNumeric* to test whether *expression* evaluates to a number.

CLng Function

CLng(*expression*)

expression   *required; Numeric or String*
    A number or a string representation of a number

Named Arguments: No

Return Value: *expression* cast as a Long data type

Description: Converts *expression* to a long integer; any fractional element of *expression* is rounded. When the fractional part is exactly .5, *CLng* always rounds it to the nearest even number. If *expression* is not numeric or is outside the range of the Long data type, an exception is generated. Use *IsNumeric* to test whether *expression* evaluates to a number.

CObj Function

CObj(*expression*)

expression   *required; any*
Expression to be converted to type Object

Named Arguments: No

Return Value: *expression* cast as an Object data type

Description: Converts any expression that can be interpreted as an object to Object. *expression* can be any data type, including a strongly typed object, as the following code fragment illustrates:

```
Dim oSomeClass As New CSomeClass
Dim oObj As Object
oObj = CObj(oSomeClass)
```

CSng Function

CSng(*expression*)

expression   *required; Numeric or String*
The range of *expression* is −3.402823E38 to −1.401298E-45 for negative values, and 1.401298E-45 to 3.402823E38 for positive values.

Named Arguments: No

Return Value: *expression* cast as a Single data type

Description: Returns a single-precision number.

CStr Function

CStr(*expression*)

expression   *required; any*
Any numeric, date, string, or Boolean expression

Named Arguments: No

Return Value: *expression* converted to a string

Description: Returns a string representation of *expression*.

CType Function

CType(*expression, typename*)

expression   *required; any*
   The data item to be converted

typename   *required; Keyword*
   The data type, object type, structure, or interface to which
   expression is to be converted

Named Arguments: No

Return Value: *expression* cast as a *typename* interface, object,
structure, or data type

Description: Converts an expression to the specified data type if
possible; *expression* can be any data, object, structure, or interface type. *typename* can be any data type (such as Boolean, Byte,
Decimal, Long, Short, String, etc.), structure type, object type, or
interface that can be used with the As clause in a Dim statement. If
the function fails, or if the converted value of *expression* is outside
the range allowed by *typename*, an InvalidCastException exception occurs.

DateValue Function   Microsoft.VisualBasic.DateAndTime

DateValue(*stringdate*)

stringdate   *required; String*
   A string containing any of the date formats recognized by
   IsDate

Return Value: A Date that represents the date specified by the
stringdate argument

Description: Converts the string representation of a date to a Date
data type while dropping any time component. The date value is
formatted according to the short date setting defined by the
Regional Settings applet in the Control Panel. *DateValue* can
successfully recognize *stringdate* in any of the date formats recognized by *IsDate,* but the order of the day, month, and year within
stringdate must be the same as that defined by the computer's
regional settings. If you don't specify a year in your date expression, *DateValue* uses the current year from the computer's system

date. *DateValue* does not return time values in a date/time string: they simply dropped. However, if *stringdate* includes an invalid time value, an exception results.

DirectCast Function

DirectCast(*expression*, *typename*)

expression   *required; any*
    The data item to be converted

typename   *required; Keyword*
    The data type, object type, structure, or interface to which expression is to be converted

Named Arguments: No

Return Value: *expression* cast as a *typename* interface or object

Description: Converts an expression to its runtime data type, if possible; otherwise, returns an error. *expression* must be a reference type, typically a variable of type Object. *typename* can be any data type (such as Boolean, Byte, Decimal, Long, Short, String, etc.), structure type, object type, or interface. If the function fails, an InvalidCastException exception occurs.

Option Strict Statement

Option Strict [On | Off]

Description: Option Strict prevents VB from making any *implicit* narrowing data type conversions, since they may involve data loss. It also causes errors to be generated for late binding, as well as for any undeclared variables. Option Strict On implies Option Explicit On. For example:

```
Dim lNum As Long = 2455622
Dim iNum As Integer = lNum
```

converts a Long (whose value can range from 9,223,372,036,854,775,808 to 9,223,372,036,854,775,807) to an Integer (whose value can range from 2,147,483,648 to 2,147,483,647). In this case, even though no data loss would result from the narrowing, Option Strict On would still not allow the conversion and would instead generate a compiler error.

If the `Option Strict` statement is not present in a module, `Option Strict` is `Off`. The default is `Option Strict On`. In other words, the statement:

```
Option Strict On
```

is equivalent to the statement:

```
Option Strict
```

The `Option Strict` statement must appear in the declarations section of a module before any code.

The VB compiler considers the following to be narrowing conversions:

- Short, Integer, Long, Decimal, Single, Double→Byte
- Integer, Long, Decimal, Single, Double →Short
- Long, Decimal, Single, Double →Integer
- Decimal, Single, Double→Long
- Single, Double→Decimal
- Double→Single
- Integer type or wider →Any enumerated type
- String→Char
- Object→Any type
- Any base type→Any derived type
- An interface→Any type implementing the interface
- Any type→Nothing
- Conversions between Boolean and any numeric type
- Any numeric type→any enumerated type
- Conversions between a Char array and a String
- Conversions between String and any numeric, Boolean, or Date type

---

Str Function

Microsoft.VisualBasic.Conversion

`Str(number)`

number　　　　　　　　　　　　　*required; Numeric*
Any valid numeric expression or expression capable of conversion to a number

---

Return Value: A String representation of *number*

Description: Converts *number* from a numeric to a string. If the return value is positive, the *Str* function always includes a leading space in the returned string for the sign of *number*.

TimeValue Function

TimeValue(*stringtime*)

stringtime   *required; String*
    Any valid string representation of a time

Return Value: A Date containing the time specified by the *string time* argument, with the date set to January 1 of the year 1 CE.

Description: Converts the string representation of a time to a Date type containing the time. *stringtime* can be in any time format recognized by the *IsDate* function. Both 12- and 24-hour clock formats are valid. The Date value returned by time is formatted based on the system's regional settings. If stringtime is invalid or is Nothing, an exception is raised.

Val Function

Val(*expression*)

expression   *required; String or Char*
    Any string representation of a number

Return Value: A Double able to hold the number contained in *expression*

Description: Converts a string representation of a number into a Double. The *Val* function starts reading the string with the leftmost character and stops at the first character that it does not recognize as being part of a valid number. For example, the statement:

```
iNumber = Val("1A1")
```

returns 1.

&O and &H (the octal and hexadecimal prefixes) are recognized by the *Val* function and the period (.) is recognized as a decimal delimitor. Currency symbols, such as $ and £, and delimiters, such as commas, are not recognized. Prior to processing *expression*, *Val* removes spaces, tabs, and line-feed characters.

ValDec Function   Microsoft.VisualBasic.Conversion

ValDec(*expression*)

expression   required; String or Char
    Any string representation of a number

Return Value: A Decimal able to hold the number contained in *expression*

Description: Converts a string representation of a number into a Decimal. The *ValDec* function starts reading the string with the leftmost character and stops at the first character that it does not recognize as being part of a valid number. For example, the statement:

```
iNumber = ValDec("1A1")
```

returns 1.

&O and &H (the octal and hexadecimal prefixes) are recognized by the *ValDec* function. Currency symbols, such as $ and £, and delimiters, such as commas, are not recognized as numbers by the *ValDec* function. The *ValDec* function only recognizes the period (.) as a decimal delimiter. Prior to processing *expression*, *ValDec* removes spaces, tabs, and line-feed characters.

Other Conversion

Fix Function   Microsoft.VisualBasic.Conversion

Fix(*number*)

number   required; Double or any numeric expression
    A number whose integer portion is to be returned

Return Value: A number of the same data type as *number* whose value is the integer portion of *number*

Description: For nonnegative numbers, *Fix* returns the floor of the number (the largest integer less than or equal to *number*). For negative numbers, *Fix* returns the ceiling of the number (the smallest integer greater than or equal to *number*). If *number* is Nothing, *Fix* returns Nothing.

The operation of *Int* and *Fix* are identical when dealing with positive numbers: numbers are rounded down to the next lowest whole number. For example, both Int(3.14) and Fix(3.14) return 3. If *number* is negative, *Fix* removes its fractional part, thereby returning the next greater whole number. For example, Fix(-3.667) returns –3. This contrasts with *Int*, which returns the negative integer less than or equal to number (or –4, in the case of our example).

Hex Function   Microsoft.VisualBasic.Conversion

Hex(*number*)

number   *required; Numeric or String*
   A valid numeric or string expression

Return Value: String representing the hexadecimal value of *number*

Description: Converts a number to its hexadecimal (base 16) equivalent. If *number* contains a fractional part, it will be automatically rounded to the nearest whole number before the *Hex* function is evaluated. *number* must evaluate to a numeric expression that ranges from –2,147,483,648 to 2,147,483,647. If the argument is outside of this range, an exception results. The return value of *Hex* is dependent upon the value and type of *number*:

number	Return value
Nothing	Zero (0)
Any other number	Up to eight hexadecimal characters

Int Function   Microsoft.VisualBasic.Conversion

Int(*number*)

number   *required; any valid numeric data type*
   The number to be processed

Return Value: Returns a value of the data type passed to it

Description: Returns the integer portion of a number. The fractional part of *number* is removed, and the resulting integer value is returned. *Int* does not round *number* to the nearest whole number. For example, Int(100.9) returns 100. If *number* is negative, *Int* returns the first negative integer less than or equal to *number*. For example, Int(-10.1) returns –11.

Oct Function
Microsoft.VisualBasic.Conversion

Oct(*number*)

number   required; *Numeric or String*
    A valid numeric or string expression

Return Value: String

Description: Returns the octal value of a given number. If *number* is not already a whole number, it is rounded to the nearest whole number before being evaluated. If *number* is Nothing, an error occurs. *Oct* returns up to 11 octal characters.

QBColor Function
Microsoft.VisualBasic.Information

QBColor(*color*)

color   required; *Integer*
    A whole number between 0–15

Return Value: Long

Description: Returns a Long integer representing the RGB system color code. *color* can have any of the following values:

0	Black	8	Gray
1	Blue	9	Light Blue
2	Green	10	Light Green
3	Cyan	11	Light Cyan
4	Red	12	Light Red
5	Magenta	13	Light Magenta
6	Yellow	14	Light Yellow
7	White	15	Bright White

RGB Function   Microsoft.VisualBasic.Information

RGB(*red*, *green*, *blue*)

red   *required; Integer*
    A number between 0 and 255, inclusive

green   *required; Integer*
    A number between 0 and 255, inclusive

blue   *required; Integer*
    A number between 0 and 255, inclusive

Return Value: An Integer representing the RGB color value

Description: Returns a system color code that can be assigned to object color properties. The RGB color value represents the relative intensity of the red, green, and blue components of a pixel that produces a specific color on the display. The *RGB* function assumes any argument greater than 255 to be 255.

The following table demonstrates how the individual color values combine to create certain colors:

Color	Red	Green	Blue
Black	0	0	0
Blue	0	0	255
Green	0	255	0
Red	255	0	0
White	255	255	255

Date and Time

DateAdd Function   Microsoft.VisualBasic.DateAndTime

DateAdd(*interval*, *number*, *datevalue*)

interval   *required; String or* DateInterval *enum*
    The interval of time to add

number   *required; Double*
An expression denoting the number of time intervals you
want to add (it can be positive or negative)

datevalue   *required; Date, or an expression*
capable of conversion to a date
The starting date to which the interval is to be added

Return Value: A past or future Date that reflects the result of the
addition

Description: Returns a Date representing the result of adding (or
subtracting, if *number* is negative) a given number of time periods
to or from a given date. For instance, you can calculate the date
178 months before today's date, or the date and time 12,789
minutes from now.

interval can be one of the following literal strings:

yyyy	Year
q	Quarter
m	Month
y	Day of year
d	Day
w	Weekday
ww	Week
h	Hour
n	Minute
s	Second

interval can also be a member of the DateInterval enum:

```
Enum DateInterval
    Day
    DayOfYear
    Hour
    Minute
    Month
    Quarter
    Second
    Week
    Weekday
    WeekOfYear
End Enum
```

If *number* is positive, the result will be in the future; if *number* is negative, the result will be in the past. (The meaning of "future" and "past" here is relative to *datevalue*.)

The *DateAdd* function has a built-in calendar algorithm to prevent it from returning an invalid date. You can add 10 minutes to 31 December 1999 23:55, and *DateAdd* automatically recalculates all elements of the date to return a valid date, in this case 1 January 2000 00:05. This includes leap years; the calendar algorithm takes the presence of 29 February into account for leap years.

DateDiff Function   Microsoft.VisualBasic.DateAndTime

DateDiff(*interval*, *date1*, *date2*[, *dayofweek*[, *weekofyear*]])

interval   *required; String or* DateInterval *enum*
    Specifies the time unit used to express the difference between *date1* and *date2*

date1, date2   *required; Date or a literal date*
    The starting and ending dates, whose difference is computed as *date2- date1*

dayofweek   *optional;* FirstDayOfWeek *enum*
    A member of the FirstDayOfWeek enum

weekofyear   *optional;* FirstWeekOfYear *enum*
    A member of the FirstWeekOfYear enum

Return Value: A Long specifying the number of time intervals between the two dates

Description: Calculates the number of time intervals between two dates. For example, you can use the function to determine how many days there are between 1 January 1980 and 31 May 1998.

interval can be one of the following literal strings:

yyyy	Year
q	Quarter
m	Month
y	Day of year
d	Day
w	Weekday

ww	Week
h	Hour
n	Minute
s	Second

interval can also be a member of the DateInterval enum:

```
Enum DateInterval
    Day
    DayOfYear
    Hour
    Minute
    Month
    Quarter
    Second
    Week
    Weekday
    WeekOfYear
End Enum
```

When *interval* is Weekday or "w", *DateDiff* returns the number of weeks between the two dates. If *date1* falls on a Monday, *Date-Diff* counts the number of Mondays until *date2*. It counts *date2*, but not *date1*. If *interval* is Week or "ww", however, *DateDiff* returns the number of calendar weeks between the two dates. It counts the number of Sundays between *date1* and *date2*. *DateDiff* counts *date2* if it falls on a Sunday, but it doesn't count *date1*, even if it does fall on a Sunday.

DatePart Function   Microsoft.VisualBasic.DateAndTime

```
DatePart(interval, datevalue[,firstdayofweekvalue[, _
    firstweekofyearvalue]])
```

interval   *required; String or* DateInterval *enum*
   Defines the part of the date/time to extract from *datevalue*

datevalue   *required; Date, or an expression capable of conversion to a date*
   The Date value to evaluate

firstdayofweekvalue   *optional;* FirstDayOfWeek *enum*
   A member of the FirstDayOfWeek enum

firstweekofyearvalue   *optional;* FirstWeekOfYear *enum*
   A member of the FirstWeekOfYear enum

Return Value: An Integer containing the specified part

Description: Extracts an individual component of the date or time (like the month or the second) from a date/time value. The *DatePart* function returns an Integer containing the specified portion of the given date. *DatePart* is a single function encapsulating the individual *Year*, *Month*, *Day*, *Hour*, *Minute*, and *Second* functions.

interval can be one of the following literal strings:

yyyy	Year
q	Quarter
m	Month
y	Day of year
d	Day
w	Weekday
ww	Week
h	Hour
n	Minute
s	Second

interval can also be a member of the DateInterval enum:

```
Enum DateInterval
    Day
    DayOfYear
    Hour
    Minute
    Month
    Quarter
    Second
    Week
    Weekday
    WeekOfYear
End Enum
```

The *firstdayofweekvalue* argument can be any of the following members of the FirstDayOfWeek enumeration:

```
Enum FirstDayOfWeek
    System       'uses first day of week
                 'setting on local system
```

```
        Sunday
        Monday
        Tuesday
        Wednesday
        Thursday
        Friday
        Saturday
    End Enum
```

The *firstdayofweekvalue* argument affects only calculations that use either the Week (or "w") or Weekday (or "ww") *interval* values.

The *firstweekofyearvalue* argument can be any of the following members of the FirstWeekOfYear enumeration:

FirstWeekOfYear constant	Value	Description
System	0	Uses the local system setting
Jan1	1	Starts with the week in which January 1 occurs (the default value)
FirstFourDays	2	Starts with the first week that has at least four days in the new year
FirstFullWeek	3	Starts with the first full week of the year

DateSerial Function   Microsoft.VisualBasic.DateAndTime

DateSerial(*year, month, day*)

year   required; Integer
    Number between 100 and 9999, inclusive, or a numeric expression

month   required; Integer
    Any numeric expression between 1 and 12 to express the month

day   required; Integer
    Any numeric expression between 1 and 31 to express the day

Return Value: A Date representing the date specified by the arguments

Description: Returns a Date whose value is specified by the three date components (year, month, and day).

For the function to succeed, all three components must be present, and all must be numeric values. The value returned by the function takes the short date format defined by the Regional Settings applet in the Control Panel of the client machine.

If the value of a particular element exceeds its normal limits, *DateSerial* adjusts the date accordingly. For example, DateSerial(96,2,31)—February 31, 1996—returns March 2, 1996.

You can specify expressions or formulas that evaluate to individual date components as parameters to *DateSerial*. For example, DateSerial(98,10+9,23) returns 23 March 1999. This makes it easier to use *DateSerial* to form dates whose individual elements are unknown at design time or that are created on the fly as a result of user input.

DateString Property   Microsoft.VisualBasic.DateAndTime

DateString( )

Return Value: A String representing the current system date in the format "mm-dd- yyyy"

Description: Returns or sets a string representing the current system date. The allowed formats for setting the date are "m-d-yyyy," "m-d-y," "m/d/yyyy," and "m/d/y."

Day Function   Microsoft.VisualBasic.DateAndTime

Day(*datevalue*)

datevalue   *required; Date or literal date*
    Date whose day number is to be extracted

Return Value: An Integer from 1 to 31, representing the day of the month

Description: Returns an Integer ranging from 1 to 31, representing the day of the month of *datevalue*. The range of *datevalue* is 1/1/1 to 12/31/9999.

With Option Strict On, you must first convert *datevalue* to a Date data type before passing it to the *Day* function. You can use the *CDate* function for this purpose.

If the day portion of *datevalue* is outside of its valid range, the function generates an exception. This is also true if the day and month portion of *datevalue* is 2/29 for a non-leap year.

GetTimer Function   Microsoft.VisualBasic.VBMath

GetTimer( )

Return Value: A Double indicating the number of seconds

Description: Returns the number of seconds since midnight.

Hour Function   Microsoft.VisualBasic.DateAndTime

Hour(*timevalue*)

timevalue   *required; Date*
    Date variable or literal date whose hour component is to be
    extracted

Return Value: An Integer from 0 to 23, specifying the hour of the day

Description: Extracts the hour element from a time expression. Regardless of the time format passed to *Hour*, the return value will be a whole number between 0 and 23, representing the hour of a 24-hour clock. If *time* contains Nothing, 0 is returned, so be careful here to check for Nothing.

Minute Function   Microsoft.VisualBasic.DateAndTime

Minute(*TimeValue*)

TimeValue   *required; Date*
    Date variable or literal date

Return Value: An Integer between 0 and 59, representing the minute of the hour

Description: Extracts the minute component from a given date/time expression

If *TimeValue* is not a valid date/time expression, the function generates an exception. To prevent this, use the *IsDate* function to check the argument before calling the *Minute* function. If *TimeValue* contains Nothing, 0 is returned, so be careful here to check for Nothing.

Month Function
Microsoft.VisualBasic.DateAndTime

Month(*datevalue*)

datevalue   *required; Date*
   Date variable or literal date whose month component is to be extracted.

Return Value: An Integer between 1 and 12

Description: Returns an integer representing the month of the year of a given date expression. If *datevalue* contains Nothing, *Month* returns Nothing.

MonthName Function
Microsoft.VisualBasic.DateAndTime

MonthName(*month* [, *abbreviate*])

month   *required; Integer*
   The ordinal number of the month, from 1 to 12

abbreviate   *optional; Boolean*
   A flag to indicate if an abbreviated month name should be returned

Return Value: String containing the name of the specified month

Description: Returns the month name of a given month. For example, a *month* of 1 returns January or (if *abbreviate* is True) Jan. The default value for *abbreviate* is False.

Now Property
Microsoft.VisualBasic.DateAndTime

Now( )

Return Value: A Date containing the current system date and time

Description: Returns the current date and time based on the system setting. The date returned by Now takes the Windows General Date format based on the locale settings of the local computer. The U.S. setting for General Date is mm/dd/yy hh:mm:ss. The Now property is read-only.

Second Function   Microsoft.VisualBasic.DateAndTime

Second(*timevalue*)

timevalue   required; Date
    Date variable or literal date

Return Value: An Integer in the range 0 to 59, specifying the
second in *timevalue*

Description: Extracts the seconds from a given time expression. If
the time expression time is Nothing, the *Second* function returns 0.

TimeOfDay Property   Microsoft.VisualBasic.DateAndTime

TimeOfDay

Return Value: Date value giving the current system time

Description: Sets or returns the current system time.

Timer Property   Microsoft.VisualBasic.DateAndTime

Timer

Return Value: Double representing the number of seconds that
have elapsed since midnight

Description: Returns the number of seconds since midnight.

TimeSerial Function   Microsoft.VisualBasic.DateAndTime

TimeSerial(*hour, minute, second*)

hour   required; Integer
    A number in the range 0 to 23

minute   required; Integer
    Any valid integer

second   required; Integer
    Any valid integer

Return Value: A Date representing the time specified by the arguments to the function

Description: Constructs a valid time given a number of hours, minutes, and seconds. Any of the arguments can be specified as relative values or expressions. The *hour* argument requires a 24-hour clock format; however, the returned time is determined by the system's regional settings.

If any value is greater than the normal range for the time unit to which it relates, the next higher time unit is increased accordingly. For example, a *second* argument of 125 will be evaluated as 2 minutes, 5 seconds.

If any value is less than zero, the next higher time unit is decreased accordingly. For example, TimeSerial(2,-1,30) returns 01:59:30.

TimeString Property   Microsoft.VisualBasic.DateAndTime

TimeString( )

Return Value: String representing the current system time

Description: The TimeString property returns the current system time in the format determined by the system's regional settings. You can use any time format recognized by *IsDate* when setting the time using the TimeString property.

The string returned by the TimeString property also includes an invalid date, 01/01/0001. It can be eliminated with the *Format* or *FormatDateTime* function as follows:

```
Format(TimeOfDay( ), "Long Time")
FormatDateTime(TimeOfDay( ), DateFormat.LongTime)
```

TimeValue Function

See "TimeValue Function" entry under "Data Type Conversions."

Weekday Function   Microsoft.VisualBasic.DateAndTime

Weekday(*datevalue*, [*dayofweek*])

date   required; *Date or valid date expression*
    Any valid date expression

dayofweek   optional; *Constant of* FirstDayOfWeek *enumeration*
    A constant indicating the first day of the week

Return Value: Integer

Description: Determines the day of the week of a given date. The default for *dayofweek* is FirstDayOfWeek.Sunday.

To determine the day of the week, think of the day specified by *dayofweek* as day 1, and the value returned by the function as indicating the day relative to day 1. Then, for example, if the return value of *WeekDay* is 2, this specifies the day following *dayofweek*. A return value of 1 specifies *dayofweek*. A return value of 7 specifies the day before *dayofweek*.

The members of the FirstDayOfWeek enumeration are:

Constant	Value	Description
Sunday	1	Sunday
Monday	2	Monday
Tuesday	3	Tuesday
Wednesday	3	Wednesday
Thursday	4	Thursday
Friday	5	Friday
Saturday	6	Saturday
Sunday	7	Sunday

Passing a value of 0 as the *dayofweek* argument uses the system's locale settings to determine the first day of the week.

WeekdayName Function   Microsoft.VisualBasic.DateAndTime

WeekdayName(*Weekday*, [*abbreviate* [, *FirstDayOfWeekValue*]])

Weekday   *required; Long*
    The ordinal number of the required weekday, from 1 to 7

abbreviate   *optional; Boolean*
    Specifies whether to return the full day name or an abbreviation

FirstDayOfWeekValue   *optional;* FirstDayOfWeek *constant*
    Member of the FirstDayOfWeek enum indicating the first day of the week

Return Value: A String

Description: Returns the name of the day. *Weekday* must be a number between 1 and 7, or the function generates an ArgumentException error.

The default value of *abbreviate* is False. For a list of the members of the FirstDayOfWeek enumeration, see the "Weekday Function" entry. The default value of *FirstDayOfWeekValue* is FirstDayOfWeek.Monday.

Year Function   Microsoft.VisualBasic.DateAndTime

Year(*datevalue*)

datevalue   required; Date or valid date expression
Any valid date expression

Return Value: Integer

Description: Returns an integer representing the year in a given date expression. If OptionStrict is off and *datevalue* contains Nothing, *Year* returns 1. For example:

```
Dim oDat As Object
Console.Writeline(Year(sDat))          ' Displays 1
```

If *datevalue* is a date literal (a date delimited with the # symbol), the year must contain four digits.

Declaration

Class... End Class Statement

```
[accessmodifier] [Shadows] [inheritability] Class Name
    statements
End Class
```

accessmodifier   optional; Keyword
The possible values of *accessmodifier* are Public, Private, and Friend

Shadows   optional; Keyword
Indicates that the *Name* class shadows any element of this same name in a base class

---

inheritability   optional; Keyword
> One of the keywords, MustInherit or NotInheritable, must be used. MustInherit specifies that objects of this class cannot be created, but that objects of derived classes can be created. NotInheritable specifies that this class cannot be used as a base class

Name   required; String literal
> The name of the class

Description: Defines a class and delimits the statements that define that class' variables, properties, and methods.

If the Inherits or Implements statements appear in a class module, they must appear before any other statements in the module. Moreover, the Inherits keyword must appear before the Implements keyword.

Within a class code block, members are declared as Public, Private, Protected, Friend, or Protected Friend. The Dim keyword is equivalent to Private when used in class modules (but it is equivalent to Public in structures). Property declarations are automatically Public.

The Class...End Class construct can include the following elements:

Private variable or procedure declarations
> These items are accessible within the class but do not have scope outside of the class.

Public variable or procedure declarations
> Public variables are public properties of the class; Public procedures are public methods of the class.

Property declarations
> These are the public properties of the class. Default properties can be declared by using the Default keyword.

Const Statement

[*accessmodifier*] Const *constantname* [As *type*] = *constantvalue*

accessmodifier   optional; Keyword
> One of the keywords Public, Private, Protected, Friend, or Protected Friend.

---

constantname   *required; String Literal*
   The name of the constant.

type   *optional; Keyword*
   The data type; it can be Byte, Boolean, Char, Short, Integer,
   Long, Single, Double, Decimal, Date, or String, as well as any
   of the data types defined in the Base Class Library.

constantvalue   *required; Numeric or String*
   A literal, constant, or any combination of literals and constants
   that includes arithmetic or logical operators, except Is.

Description: Associates a constant value with a name. This feature
is provided to make code more readable. The name is referred to
as a *symbolic constant*.

If Option Strict is on, the data type of the constant must be
defined by using the As *type* clause.

Declare Statement

Syntax for subroutines:
```
[accessmodifier] Declare [Ansi|Unicode|Auto] Sub name_
    Lib "libname" [Alias "aliasname"] [([arglist])]
```

Syntax for functions:
```
[accessmodifier] Declare [Ansi|Unicode|Auto] Function name _
    Lib "libname" [Alias "aliasname"] [([arglist])] [As type]
```

accessmodifier   *optional; Keyword*
   accessmodifier can be any one of the following: Public,
   Private, Protected, Friend, or Protected Friend. The
   following table describes the effects of the various access
   modifiers. Note that *direct access* refers to accessing the
   member without any qualification, as in:

   ```
   classvariable = 100
   ```

   and *class/object access* refers to accessing the member through
   qualification, either with the class name or the name of an
   object of that class.

	Direct access scope	Class/object access scope
Private	Declaring class	Declaring class
Protected	All derived classes	Declaring class
Friend	Derived in-project classes	Declaring project
Protected Friend	All derived classes	Declaring project
Public	All derived classes	All projects

Ansi   *optional; Keyword*

Converts all strings to ANSI values.

Unicode   *optional; Keyword*

Converts all strings to Unicode values.

Auto   *optional; Keyword*

Converts the strings according to .NET rules based on the name of the method (or the alias name, if specified). If no modifier is specified, Auto is the default.

name   *required; String literal*

Any valid procedure name. Note that DLL entry points are case sensitive. If the *aliasname* argument is used, *name* represents the name by which the function or procedure is referenced in your code, while *aliasname* represents the name of the routine as found in the DLL.

Lib   *required; Keyword*

Indicates that a DLL or code resource contains the procedure being declared.

libname   *required; String literal*

Name of the DLL or code resource that contains the declared procedure.

Alias   *optional; Keyword*

Indicates that the procedure being called has another name in the DLL. This is useful when the external procedure name is the same as a keyword. You can also use Alias when a DLL procedure has the same name as a public variable, constant, or any other procedure in the same scope. Alias is also useful if any characters in the DLL procedure name aren't allowed by VB.NET naming conventions.

aliasname   *optional; String literal*

    Name of the procedure in the DLL or code resource. If the first character is not a number sign (#), *aliasname* is the name of the procedure's entry point in the DLL. If # is the first character, all characters that follow must indicate the ordinal number of the procedure's entry point.

arglist   *optional*

    List of variables representing arguments that are passed to the procedure when it is called.

type   *optional; Keyword*

    Data type of the value returned by a Function procedure; may be Byte, Boolean, Char, Short, Integer, Long, Single, Double, Decimal, Date, String, Object, or any user-defined type. Arrays of any type cannot be returned, but an Object containing an array can.

Description: Used at module level to declare references to external procedures in a dynamic-link library (DLL).

The data type you use in the As clause following *arglist* must match that returned by the function.

Dim Statement

```
[Shared] [Shadows] [readonly] Dim_
[WithEvents] varname[([subscripts])]_
[As [New] type] [= initexpr]
```

Shared   *optional; Keyword*

    Indicates the variable is not associated with any particular class instance but is accessible directly using the class name and is therefore "shared" by all class instances.

Shadows   *optional; Keyword*

    Indicates that the variable shadows any programming elements (variables, procedures, enums, constants, etc.) of the same name in a base class.

WithEvents   *optional; Keyword*

    In an object variable definition, indicates that the object will receive event notification

varname   *required*

    The name of the variable

subscripts   *optional*
> Dimensions of an array variable

New   *optional; Keyword*
> Keyword that creates an instance of an object

type   *optional unless* Option Strict *is* On
> The data type of *varname*

initexpr   *optional*
> Any expression that provides the initial value to assign to the variable; cannot be used if an As New clause is used

Description: Declares and allocates storage space in memory for variables. The Dim statement is used either at the start of a procedure or the start of a module to declare a variable of a particular data type.

Object is the default data type created when no data type is explicitly declared.

The declaration of a nonobject variable actually creates the variable. For an object variable, the variable is not created unless the optional New statement is used. If not, then the object variable is set to Nothing and must be assigned a reference to an existing object at some later point in the code.

Variables that are not explicitly initialized by the Dim statement have the following default values:

Data type	Initial value
All numeric types	0
Boolean	False
Date	01/01/0001 12:00:00 AM
Decimal	0
Object	Nothing
String	Nothing

Enum Statement

```
accessmodifier Enum name [As type]
   membername [= constantexpression]
   membername [= constantexpression]
   ...
End Enum
```

accessmodifier   *optional; Keyword*
Possible values are Public, Private, Friend, Protected, or
Protected Friend

name   *required; String literal*
The name of the enumerated data type

membername   *required; String literal*
The name of a member of the enumerated data type

constantexpression   *optional; Long*
The value to be assigned to *membername*

type   *optional; Keyword*
The data type of the enumeration. All enumerated members
must be integers; possible values are Byte, Short, Integer, and
Long

Description: Defines an enumerated data type. All of the values of
the data type are defined by the instances of *membername*.

Friend Keyword

Description: The Friend keyword is used to declare classes,
module-level variables (but not local variables), constants,
enumerations, properties, methods, functions, and subroutines.

When the Friend keyword is used, the item being declared has
direct access scope inside of the class module in which the item is
declared, as well as in all derived classes in the same project.
However, if the item is declared using Protected Friend, then the
scope is all derived classes, including those that are in other
projects.

Function Statement

```
[ClassBehavior][AccessModifier] Function name _
        [(arglist)] [As type][()]
    [statements]
    [name = expression]
    [statements]
End Function
```

ClassBehavior   *optional; Keyword*

One of the following keywords:

Overloads

Indicates that more than one declaration of this function (with different argument signatures) exists.

Overrides

For derived classes, indicates that the function overrides the function by the same name (and argument signature) in the base class.

Overridable

Indicates that the function can be overridden in a derived class.

NotOverridable

Indicates that the function cannot be overridden in a derived class.

MustOverride

Indicates that the function must be overridden in a derived class.

Shadows

In a derived class definition, indicates that this element shadows any elements of the same name in the base class.

Shared

Makes the function callable without creating an object of the class. It is, in this strange sense, shared by all objects of the class. These are also called static functions.

AccessModifier   *optional; Keyword*

One of the following keywords: Public, Private, Protected, Friend, Protected Friend. The following table describes the effects of the various access modifiers. Note that direct access refers to accessing the member without any qualification, as in:

```
classvariable = 100
```

and class/object access refers to accessing the member through qualification, either with the class name or the name of an object of that class:

	Direct access scope	Class/object access scope
Private	Declaring class	Declaring class
Protected	All derived classes	Declaring class
Friend	Derived in-project classes	Declaring project
Protected Friend	All derived classes	Declaring project
Public	All derived classes	All projects

name   *required; String literal*

The name of the function.

arglist   *optional*

A comma-delimited list of variables to be passed to the function as arguments from the calling procedure.

arglist uses the following syntax and parts:

> [Optional] [ByVal | ByRef] [ParamArray] *varname*[( )]_
> [As *type*] [= *defaultvalue*]

Optional   *optional; Keyword*

An optional argument is one that need not be supplied when calling the function. However, all arguments following an optional one must also be optional. A ParamArray argument cannot be optional.

ByVal   *optional; Keyword*

The argument is passed by value; that is, the local copy of the variable is assigned the value of the argument. ByVal is the default method of passing variables.

ByRef   *optional; Keyword*

The argument is passed by reference; that is, the local variable is simply a reference to the argument being passed. All changes made to the local variable will be also reflected in the calling argument.

ParamArray   *optional; Keyword*

Indicates that the argument is an optional array of Objects (or a strongly typed array, if Option Strict is on) containing an arbitrary number of elements. It can only be used as the last element of the argument list and cannot be used with the ByRef or Optional keywords.

varname   *required; String literal*

The name of the local variable containing either the reference or value of the argument.

type   *optional; Keyword*

The data type of the argument.

defaultvalue   *optional; String literal*

For optional arguments, you must specify a default value.

type   *optional; Keyword*

The return data type of the function.

statements   *optional*

Program code to be executed within the function.

expression   *optional*

The value to return from the function to the calling procedure.

Description: Defines a function procedure.

If you do not include one of the access keywords, a function will be Public by default.

Option Explicit Statement

Option Explicit [On | Off]

Description: Use Option Explicit to generate a compile-time error whenever a variable that has not been declared is encountered.

In modules where the Option Explicit statement is not used, any undeclared variables are automatically cast as Objects.

The default is Option Explicit On. In other words, the statement:

    Option Explicit

---

is equivalent to:

```
Option Explicit On
```

Private Statement

```
Private [WithEvents] varname[([subscripts])] [As [New] type] _
[, [WithEvents] varname[([subscripts])] [As [New] type]] ...
```

WithEvents   *optional; Keyword*
    A keyword that denotes the object variable, *varname*, can
    respond to events triggered from within the object to which it
    refers

varname   *required; any*
    The name of the variable, following Visual Basic naming
    conventions

subscripts   *optional; Integer or Long*
    Denotes *varname* as an array and specifies the number and
    extent of array dimensions

New   *optional; Keyword*
    Used to automatically create an instance of the object referred
    to by the *varname* object variable

type   *optional; Keyword*
    Data type of the variable *varname*

Description: Used at module level to declare a private variable
and allocate the relevant storage space in memory. Private can
also be used with procedures and class modules.

Property Statement

```
[Default] [accessmodifier] [ReadOnly| WriteOnly] _
     [ClassBehavior] Property name _
     [(arglist)] [As type] [Implements interfacemember]
     Get
        [statements]
     End Get
     Set
        [statements]
     End Set
End Property
```

Default   *optional; Keyword*

> Specifies that the property is the default property. Must have both a Get and a Set block.

accessmodifier   *optional; Keyword*

> One of the keywords Public, Private, Protected, Friend, or Protected Friend.

ReadOnly   *optional; Keyword*

> Indicates that the property is read-only. Must have only a Get block. (If you try to write a Set block, VB will generate a compiler error.)

WriteOnly   *optional; Keyword*

> Indicates that the property is write-only. Must have only a Set block. (If you try to write a Get block, VB will generate a compiler error.)

ClassBehavior   *optional; Keyword*

> One of the following keywords:

> **Overloads**
>> Indicates that more than one declaration of this function (with different argument signatures) exists.

> **Overrides**
>> For derived classes, indicates that the function overrides the function by the same name (and argument signature) in the base class.

> **Overridable**
>> Indicates that the function can be overridden in a derived class.

> **NotOverridable**
>> Indicates that the function cannot be overridden in a derived class.

> **MustOverride**
>> Indicates that the function must be overridden in a derived class.

Shadows   *optional; Keyword*

> Indicates that the property shadows any element of this same name in a base class.

Shared
> Makes the function callable without creating an object of the class. It is, in this strange sense, shared by all objects of the class. These are also called static functions.

name   *required; String literal*
> The name of the property.

arglist   *optional; any*
> A comma-delimited list of variables to be passed to the property as arguments from the calling procedure.

type   *optional*
> The return data type of the property. The default is Object.

Implements *interfacename*   *optional*
> Indicates that the property implements a property by the same name in the interface named *interfacename*.

Description: Declares a class property.

Overloads and Shadows cannot be used in the same property declaration.

Property procedures are Public by default.

The Friend keyword is only valid within class modules. Friend properties are accessible to all procedures in all modules and classes within a project, but are not listed in the class library for that project. Therefore, they cannot be accessed from projects or applications outside the defining application.

Properties and procedures defined using the Friend keyword cannot be late bound.

The Default keyword can be used only in the case of parameterized properties. Typically, these are properties that either return collection objects or are implemented as property arrays.

Protected Keyword

Description: Used to declare classes and their members.

When the Protected keyword is used to modify a member declaration, the member being declared has direct access scope to the class module in which the member is declared, as well as to all derived classes in all projects. However, as far as object access is concerned, the member is considered Private; that is, it can only be accessed within the declaring class.

Declaring a class module as Protected limits all of the class' members to Protected access (or stronger if the member has further specific access restrictions).

Public Statement

```
[Overrides] [Shadows] Public [WithEvents] _
    varname[([subscripts])] [As [New] type] [, [WithEvents] _
    varname[([subscripts])] [As [New] type]] ...
```

Overrides   *optional; Keyword*
   In a derived class definition, indicates that a variable overrides a similar variable in a base class

Shadows   *optional; Keyword*
   In a derived class definition, indicates that calls to derived
   class members that are made through a base class ignore the
   shadowed implementation

WithEvents   *optional; Keyword*
   A keyword that denotes the object variable, *varname*, can
   respond to events triggered from within the object to which it
   refers

varname   *required; String literal*
   The name of the variable, which must follow Visual Basic
   naming conventions

subscripts   *optional; Numeric constant or literal*
   Denotes *varname* as an array and specifies the dimensions and
   number of elements of the array

New   *optional; Keyword*
   Used to automatically create an instance of the object referred
   to by the *varname* object variable

type   *optional*
   Data type of the variable *varname*

Description: Used at module level to declare a public variable and allocate the relevant storage space in memory.

A Public variable has both project-level scope—that is, it can be used by all procedures in all modules in the project—and, when used in a Class module, it can have scope outside the project.

The Public keyword also applies to procedures and class modules.

The behavior of a Public variable depends on where it is declared, as the following table shows:

Variable declared in...	Scope
A procedure	Illegal—this generates a compile-time error.
Code module declarations section	Variable is available to all modules within the project.
Class module declarations section	Variable is available as a property of the class to all modules within the project and to all other projects referencing the class.
Form module declarations section	Variable is available as a property of the form to all modules within the project.

Static Statement

```
Static varname[([subscripts])] [As [New] type] _
      [,varname[([subscripts])] [As [New] type]] ...
```

varname   *required; any*
    The name of the variable, following Visual Basic naming conventions

subscripts   *optional; Integer*
    Denotes *varname* as an array and specifies the dimension and upper bounds of the array

New   *optional; Keyword*
    Used to automatically create an instance of the object referred to by the object variable *varname*

type   *optional; Keyword*
    Data type of the variable *varname*

Description: Used at procedure level to declare a Static variable and to allocate the relevant storage space in memory. Static variables retain their value between calls to the procedure in which they are declared.

Structure...End Structure Statement

```
accessmodifier Structure StructureName
    [Implements interfacenames]
    variable declarations
    procedure declarations
End Structure
```

accessmodifier   *optional; Keyword*
    The possible values of *accessmodifier* are Public, Private, Friend, Protected, Protected Friend.

Implements *interfacenames*   *optional*
    Indicates that the structure implements the members of one or more interfaces

Description: Used to declare user-defined types. Structures are similar to classes, but they are value types rather than reference types.

Sub Statement

```
[ClassBehavior] [AccessModifier] Sub name [(arglist)]
    [statements]
    [Exit Sub]
    [statements]
End Sub
```

ClassBehavior   *optional; Keyword*
    One of the keywords shown in the following table:

Keyword	Description
Overloads	Indicates that more than one declaration of this subroutine exists (with different argument signatures).
Overrides	For derived classes, indicates that the subroutine overrides the subroutine by the same name (and argument signature) in the base class.

Keyword	Description
Overridable	Indicates that the subroutine can be overridden in a derived class.
NotOverridable	Indicates that the subroutine cannot be overridden in a derived class.
MustOverride	Indicates that the subroutine must be overridden in a derived class.
Shadows	In a derived class definition, indicates that calls to derived class members that are made through a base class ignore the shadowed implementation.
Shared	Callable without creating an object of the class. It is, in this strange sense, shared by all objects of the class. These are also called *static subroutines*.

AccessModifier   *optional*

Possible values are Public, Private, Friend, Protected, or Protected Friend. The following table describes the effects of the various access modifiers. Note that "direct access" refers to accessing the member without any qualification, as in:

```
classvariable = 100
```

and "class/object access" refers to accessing the member through qualification, either with the class name or the name of an object of that class.

	Direct access scope	Class/object access scope
Private	Declaring class	Declaring class
Protected	All derived classes	Declaring class
Friend	Derived in-project classes	Declaring project
Protected Friend	All derived classes	Declaring project
Public	All derived classes	All projects

name   *required; String literal*

The name of the Sub procedure.

arglist   *optional; any*

A comma-delimited list of variables to be passed to the sub procedure as arguments from the calling procedure.

arglist uses the following syntax and parts:

```
[Optional] [ByVal | ByRef] [ParamArray] varname[( )] _
    [As type] [= defaultvalue]
```

Optional   *optional; Keyword*

An optional argument is one that need not be supplied when calling the function. However, all arguments following an optional one must also be optional. A ParamArray argument cannot be optional.

ByVal   *optional; Keyword*

The argument is passed by value; that is, the local copy of the variable is assigned the value of the argument. ByVal is the default method of passing variables.

ByRef   *optional; Keyword*

The argument is passed by reference; that is, the local variable is simply a reference to the argument being passed. All changes made to the local variable will be reflected in the calling argument.

ParamArray   *optional; Keyword*

Indicates that the argument is an optional array containing an arbitrary number of elements. It can only be used as the last element of the argument list, and cannot be modified by either the ByRef or Optional keywords. If Option Strict is on, the array type must also be specified.

varname   *required; String literal*

The name of the local variable containing either the reference or value of the argument.

type   *optional; Keyword*

The data type of the argument. It can be Boolean, Byte, Char, Date, Decimal, Double, Integer, Long, Object, Short, Single, String, a user-defined type, or an object type.

defaultvalue   *optional; any*

For optional arguments, you must specify a default value.

---

statements   *optional*
    Program code to be executed within the procedure.

Description: Defines a subroutine.

If you do not include one of the *accessmodifier* keywords, a
subroutine will be Public by default.

Error Handling

Erl Property   Microsoft.VisualBasic.Information

Erl

Return Value: An Integer containing the line number

Description: Indicates the line number on which an error
occurred.

Err.Clear Method   Microsoft VisualBasic.ErrObject

Err.Clear( )

Description: Explicitly resets all the properties of the Err object
after an error has been handled.

Err.Description Property   Microsoft.VisualBasic.ErrObject

Err.Description = *string*   *To set the property*
string = Err.Description   *To return the property value*

string   *required; String*
    Any string expression

Description: A read/write property containing a short string
describing a runtime error.

Err.GetException Method   Microsoft.VisualBasic.ErrObject

Err.GetException( )

Return Value: A System.Exception object or an object inherited
from it containing the current exception

Description: Returns the Exception object associated with the current error.

Err.HelpContext Property   Microsoft.VisualBasic.ErrObject

Err.HelpContext

Description: A read/write property that either sets or returns an Integer value containing the context ID of the appropriate topic within a Help file.

Err.HelpFile Property   Microsoft.VisualBasic.ErrObject

Err.HelpFile

Description: A read/write String property that contains the fully qualified path of a Windows Help file.

Err.LastDLLError Property   Microsoft.VisualBasic.ErrObject

Err.LastDLLError

Description: A read-only property containing a system error code representing a system error produced within a DLL called from a VB program.

Err.Number Property   Microsoft.VisualBasic.ErrObject

Err.Number

Description: A read/write property containing a numeric value that represents the error code for the last error generated.

Err.Raise Method   Microsoft.VisualBasic.ErrObject

Err.Raise(*number, source, description, helpfile, helpcontext*)

number   *required; Long integer*
  A numeric identifier of the particular error

source   *optional; String*
  The name of the object or application responsible for generating the error

---

description   *optional; String*
    A useful description of the error

helpfile   *optional; String*
    The fully qualified path of a Microsoft Windows Help file
    containing help or reference material about the error

helpcontext   *optional; Long*
    The context ID within *helpfile*

Description: Generates a runtime error.

Err.Source Property   Microsoft.VisualBasic.ErrObject

Err.Source

Description: A read/write string property containing the name of
the application or the object that has generated the error.

ErrorToString Function   Microsoft.VisualBasic.Conversion

ErrorToString([*errornumber*])

errornumber   *optional; Long*
    A numeric error code

Return Value: A String containing an error message

Description: Returns the error message or error description corresponding to a particular error code.

IsError Function   Microsoft.VisualBasic.Information

IsError(*expression*)

expression   *required; Object*
    An object variable that may be an Exception object

Return Value: Boolean (True if *expression* is an Exception object,
False otherwise)

Description: Indicates whether an object is an instance of the
Exception class or one of its derived classes.

On Error Statement

```
On Error GoTo label|0|-1        Syntax 1.
On Error Resume Next            Syntax 2.
```

label   *Either* label, 0, *or* -1 *is required*
    A valid label within the subroutine

Description: Enables or disables error handling within a procedure.

If you don't use an On Error statement or a Try...Catch block in your procedure, or if you have explicitly switched off error handling, the Visual Basic runtime engine will automatically handle the error. First, it will display a dialog box containing the standard text of the error message. Second, it will terminate the application. So any error that occurs in the procedure will produce a fatal runtime error.

Resume Statement

```
Resume [0]
Resume Next
Resume label
```

Description: Used to continue program execution when an error-handling routine is complete.

Throw Statement

```
Throw exception
```

exception   *required; System Exception or a derived type*
    An Exception object representing the exception being thrown

Description: Throws an exception that can be handled using either structured exception handling (a Try...Catch block) or unstructured exception handling (the On Error statement).

Try...Catch...Finally Statement

```
Try
    tryStatements
[Catch1 [exception [As type]] [When expression]
```

```
    catchStatements1
[Exit Try]

Catch2 [exception [As type]] [When expression]
    catchStatements2
[Exit Try]
...
Catchn [exception [As type]] [When expression]
    catchStatementsn]
[Exit Try]

[Finally
    finallyStatements]
End Try
```

exception   *optional; System.Exception or a derived type*
   The exception to catch. If *exception* is omitted or if it is
   System.Exception, all exceptions will be caught. However, if
   exception is omitted, no information about the exception will
   be accessible within the Catch block.

type   *optional*
   The data type of the exception to be handled by the Catch
   block. Its value can be System.Exception or any derived type.
   If omitted, its value defaults to System.Exception, and all
   exceptions will be handled.

expression   *optional; Boolean*
   A logical expression that defines a condition under which the
   error is to be handled by the Catch block.

Description: Handles runtime errors using Structured Exception
Handling.

The *tryStatements*, which are required, constitute the Try block
and are the statements that VB monitors for errors.

The Catch blocks, of which there can be more than one, contain
code that is executed in response to VB "catching" a particular
type of error within the Try block. Thus, the Catch blocks consist
of the error-handlers for the Try block.

The phrases *exception* [As *type*] and [When *expression*] are
referred to as *filters* in the VB.NET documentation. In the former
case, *exception* is either a variable of type Exception, which is the
base class that "catches" all exceptions, or a variable of one of

Exception's derived classes. The When filter is typically used with user-defined errors.

The Exit Try statement is used to break out of any portion of a Try...Catch...Finally block.

The optional *finallyStatements* code block is executed regardless of whether an error occurs (or is caught), unless an Exit Try statement is executed.

Multiple Catch statements can be used. However, only the first Catch statement to be true is executed. This means that multiple Catch statements should be ordered from most specific to most general, with a Catch block handling errors of type System. Exception occurring last.

Filesystem

ChDir Procedure   Microsoft.VisualBasic.FileSystem

ChDir(*path*)

path   *required; String*
    The path of the directory to set as the new default directory

Description: Changes the current working (default) directory.

ChDrive Procedure   Microsoft.VisualBasic.FileSystem

ChDrive(*drive*)

drive   *required; String or Char*
    The letter of the drive (A–Z) to set as the new default drive

Description: Changes the current working (default) disk drive.

CurDir Function   Microsoft.VisualBasic.FileSystem

CurDir[(*drive*)]

drive   *optional; String or Char*
    The name of the drive

Return Value: A String containing the current path

Description: Returns the current directory of a particular drive or the default drive.

If no drive is specified or if *drive* is a zero-length string (""), *CurDir* returns the path for the current drive.

drive can be the single-letter drive name with or without a colon (i.e., both "C" and "C:" are valid values for *drive*).

If *drive* is invalid, the function will generate an *10Exception* exception.

Because *CurDir* can only accept a single-character string, you cannot use network drive names, share names, or UNC drive names.

Dir Function   Microsoft.VisualBasic.FileSystem

Dir[(*pathname*[, *attributes*])]

pathname   *optional; String*
    A string expression that defines a path, which may contain a drive name, a folder name, and a filename

attributes   *optional; Numeric or Constant of*
                                          the FileAttribute *enumeration*
    The file attributes to be matched

Return Value: String

Description: Returns the name of a single file or folder matching the pattern and attribute passed to the function.

A zero-length string ("") is returned if a matching file is not found.

Possible values for *attributes* are:

FileAttribute enumeration	Value	Description
Normal	0	Normal (not hidden and not a system file)
ReadOnly	1	Read-only file
Hidden	2	Hidden
System	4	System file
Volume	8	Volume label; if specified, all other attributes are ignored

FileAttribute enumeration	Value	Description
Directory	16	Directory or folder
Archive	32	Archive
Alias	64	Alias or link

FileCopy Procedure

Microsoft.VisualBasic.FileSystem

FileCopy(*source*, *destination*)

source *required; String*
    The name of the source file to be copied

destination *required; String*
    The name and location of the file when copied

Return Value: None

Description: Copies a file.

FileDateTime Function

Microsoft.VisualBasic.FileSystem

FileDateTime(*pathname*)

pathname *required; String*
    The filename, along with an optional drive and path

Return Value: A Date containing the date and time at which the specified file was created or last modified

Description: Obtains the date and time at which a particular file was created or last modified (whichever is later).

GetAttr Function

Microsoft.VisualBasic.FileSystem

GetAttr(*pathname*)

pathname *required; String*
    Filename and an optional pathname

Return Value: An integer representing the sum of the following constants or members of the FileAttribute enumeration, which reflect the attributes set for the file:

FileAttribute Numeration	Constant	Value	Description
Normal	VbNormal	0	Normal
ReadOnly	VbReadOnly	1	Read-only
Hidden	VbHidden	2	Hidden
System	VbSystem	4	System
Directory	VbDirectory	16	Directory or folder
Archive	VbArchive	32	File has changed since last backup

Description: Determines which attributes have been set for a file or directory

---

Kill Procedure

Microsoft.VisualBasic.FileSystem

Kill(*pathname*)

pathname   *required; String*
The file or files to be deleted

Description: Deletes a file from disk. The ? and * wildcard characters can be used to specify multiple files.

MkDir Procedure

Microsoft.VisualBasic.FileSystem

MkDir(*path*)

path   *required; String*
The name of the folder to be created

Description: Creates a new folder.

Rename Procedure

Microsoft.VisualBasic.FileSystem

Rename(*oldpath*, *newpath*)

oldpath   *required; String*
The current filename and optional path

newpath   *required; String*
The new filename and optional path

Description: Renames a disk file or folder.

RmDir Procedure   Microsoft.VisualBasic.FileSystem

RmDir(*path*)

path   *required; String*
    The path of the folder to be removed

Description: Removes a folder.

SetAttr Procedure   Microsoft.VisualBasic.FileSystem

SetAttr(*pathname, attributes*)

pathname   *required; String*
    The name of the file or directory whose attributes are to be set

attributes   *required;* FileAttribute *enumeration*
    Numeric expression, FileAttribute enumerated constant, or
    global VB constant specifying the attributes

Description: Changes the attribute properties of a file.

You can use any sum of the following constants to set the
attributes of a file:

Constant	Value	Description
VbNormal	0	Normal
VbReadOnly	1	Read-only
VbHidden	2	Hidden
VbSystem	4	System
VbArchive	32	File has changed since last backup

Each global constant has a corresponding constant in the
FileAttribute enumeration. For example, vbNormal is identical to
FileAttribute.Normal. The file-attribute constants vbDirectory,
vbAlias, and vbVolume cannot be used when assigning attributes.

File-attributes constants can be Ored to set more than one
attribute at the same time. For example:

```
SetAttr "SysFile.Dat", FileAttribute.System Or
FileAttribute.Hidden
```

Unlock Procedure

Microsoft.VisualBasic.FileSystem

```
Unlock(filenumber[, record)
Unlock(filenumber[, fromrecord[, torecord]])
```

filenumber   *required; Integer*
   Any valid file number

record   *required; Long*
   The record or byte number at which to commence the lock

fromrecord   *required; Long*
   The first record or byte number to lock

torecord   *required; Long*
   The last record or byte number to lock

Description: Use the *Unlock* procedure in situations where more than one part of your program may need read and write access to the same data file. The *Unlock* procedure removes a lock that the *Lock* procedure placed on a section of the file or the whole file.

Write Procedure

Microsoft.VisualBasic.FileSystem

```
Write(filenumber, output)
```

filenumber   *required; Integer*
   Any valid file number

output   *required; Object (any)*
   A comma-delimited list of expressions or a ParamArray to be written to the file.

Named Arguments: No

Description: Writes data to a sequential file

WriteLine Procedure

Microsoft.VisualBasic.FileSystem

```
WriteLine(filenumber, [output])
```

filenumber   *required; Integer*
   Any valid file number

output   *optional; Object (any)*
   A comma-delimited list of expressions or a ParamArray to be written to the file

Named Arguments: No

Description: Writes data to a sequential file and then adds a line-feed character combination

Financial

DDB Function   Microsoft.VisualBasic.Financial

DDB(*cost*, *salvage*, *life*, *period*[, *factor*])

cost   *required; Double*
    The initial cost of the asset

salvage   *required; Double*
    The value of the asset at the end of *life*

life   *required; Double*
    Length of life of the asset

period   *required; Double*
    Period for which the depreciation is to be calculated

factor   *optional; Double*
    The rate at which the asset balance declines. If omitted, 2 (double-declining method) is assumed; however, the documentation doesn't mention what other values are supported or what they mean

Return Value: Double representing the depreciation of an asset

Description: Returns a Double representing the depreciation of an asset for a specific time period. This is done using the double-declining balance method or another method that you specify using the *factor* argument.

The double-declining balance calculates depreciation at a differential rate, which varies inversely with the age of the asset. Depreciation is highest at the beginning of an asset's life and declines over time.

FV Function   Microsoft.VisualBasic.Financial

FV(*rate*, *nper*, *pmt*[, *pv* [, *due*]])

rate   *required; Double*
> The interest rate per period

nper   *required; Integer*
> The number of payment periods in the annuity

pmt   *required; Double*
> The payment made in each period

pv   *optional; Variant*
> The present value of the loan or annuity

due   *optional; Constant of the* DueDate *enumeration*
> Specifies whether payments are due at the start or the end of
> the period. The value can be DueDate.BegOfPeriod or DueDate.
> EndOfPeriod (the default).

Return Value: A Double specifying the future value of an annuity

Description: Calculates the future value of an annuity (either an
investment or loan) based on a regular number of payments of a
fixed value and a static interest rate over the period of the annuity.

IPmt Function   Microsoft.VisualBasic.Financial

IPmt(*rate, per, nper, pv*[, *fv*[, *due*]])

rate   *required; Double*
> The interest rate per period.

per   *required; Double*
> The period for which a payment is to be computed.

nper   *required; Double*
> The total number of payment periods.

pv   *required; Double*
> The present value of a series of future payments.

fv   *optional; Double*
> The future value or cash balance after the final payment. If
> omitted, the default value is 0.

due   *optional;* DueDate *enumeration*
> A value indicating when payments are due. DueDate.
> EndOfPeriod (or 0) indicates that payments are due at the end
> of the payment period; DueDate. BegOfPeriod (or 1) indicates

that payments are due at the beginning of the period. If omitted, the default value is DueDate.EndOfPeriod.

Return Value: A Double representing the interest payment

Description: Computes the interest payment for a given period of an annuity based on periodic, fixed payments and a fixed interest rate. An annuity is a series of fixed cash payments made over a period of time. It can be either a loan payment or an investment.

IRR Function   Microsoft.VisualBasic.Financial

IRR(*valuearray*( )[, *guess*])

valuearray( )   *required; array of Double*
  An array of cash flow values

guess   *optional; Double*
  Estimated value to be returned by the function

Return Value: A Double representing the internal rate of return

Description: Calculates the internal rate of return for a series of periodic cash flows (payments and receipts).

The internal rate of return is the interest rate generated by an investment consisting of payments and receipts that occur at regular intervals. It is generally compared to a "hurdle rate," or a minimum return, to determine whether a particular investment should be made.

MIRR Function   Microsoft.VisualBasic.Financial

MIRR(*valuearray*( ), *financerate*, *reinvestrate*)

valuearray( )   *required; Array of Double*
  An array of cash flow values

financerate   *required; Double*
  The interest rate paid as the cost of financing

reinvestrate   *required; Double*
  The interest rate received on gains from cash investment

Return Value: A Double representing the modified internal rate of return

---

Description: Calculates the modified internal rate of return, which is the internal rate of return when payments and receipts are financed at different rates.

NPer Function   Microsoft.VisualBasic.Financial

NPer(*rate*, *pmt*, *pv* [, *fv* [, *due*]])

rate   *required; Double*
    The interest rate per period.

pmt   *required; Double*
    The payment to be made each period.

pv   *required; Double*
    The present value of the series of future payments or receipts.

fv   *optional; Double*
    The future value of the series of payments or receipts. If omitted, the default value is 0.

due   *optional; DueDate enumeration*
    A value indicating when payments are due. DueDate. EndOfPeriod (0) indicates that payments are due at the end of the payment period, and DueDate. BegOfPeriod (1) indicates that payments are due at the beginning of the period. If omitted, the default value is 0.

Return Value: A Double indicating the number of payments

Description: Determines the number of payment periods for an annuity based on fixed periodic payments and a fixed interest rate.

NPV Function   Microsoft.VisualBasic.Financial

NPV(*rate*, *valuearray*( ))

rate   *required; Double*
    The discount rate over the period, expressed as a decimal

valuearray()   *required; Double*
    An array of cash flow values

Return Value: A Double specifying the net present value

Description: Calculates the net present value of an investment based on a series of periodic variable cash flows (payments and receipts) and a discount rate.

The *net present value* is the value today of a series of future cash flows discounted at some rate back to the first day of the investment period.

Pmt Function   Microsoft.VisualBasic.Financial

Pmt(*rate*, *nper*, *pv*[, *fv*[, *due*]])

rate   required; *Double*
  The interest rate per period.

nper   required; *Double*
  The total number of payment periods.

pv   required; *Double*
  The present value of the series of future payments.

fv   optional; *Double*
  The future value or cash balance after the final payment.

due   optional; DueDate *enumeration*
  A value indicating when payments are due. EndOfPeriod (0) indicates that payments are due at the end of the payment period; BegOfPeriod (1) indicates that payments are due at the beginning of the period. If omitted, the default value is 0.

Return Value: A Double representing the monthly payment

Description: Calculates the payment for an annuity based on periodic, fixed payments and a fixed interest rate. An annuity can be either a loan or an investment.

PPmt Function   Microsoft.VisualBasic.Financial

PPmt(*rate*, *per*, *nper*, *pv*[, *fv*[, *due*]])

rate   required; *Double*
  The interest rate per period.

per   required; *Double*
  The period for which a payment is to be computed.

---

nper   *required; Double*
>   The total number of payment periods.

pv   *required; Double*
>   The present value of a series of future payments.

fv   *optional; Object*
>   The future value or cash balance after the final payment. If
>   omitted, the default value is 0.

due   *optional;* DueDate *enumeration*
>   A value indicating when payments are due. It can be either
>   DueDate.EndOfPeriod, for payments due at the end of the
>   period, or DueDate.BegOfPeriod for payments due at the begin-
>   ning of the period. The default value is DueDate.EndOfPeriod.

Return Value: A Double representing the principal paid in a given
payment

Description: Computes the payment of principal for a given
period of an annuity, based on periodic, fixed payments and a
fixed interest rate. An annuity is a series of fixed cash payments
made over a period of time. It can be either a loan payment or an
investment.

PV Function   Microsoft.VisualBasic.Financial

PV(*rate, nper, pmt*[, *fv* [, *due*]])

rate   *required; Double*
>   The interest rate per period

nper   *required; Integer*
>   The number of payment periods in the annuity

pmt   *required; Double*
>   The payment made in each period

fv   *optional; Double*
>   The future value of the loan or annuity

due   *optional; DueDate*
>   Either DueDate.BegOfPeriod or DueDate.EndOfPeriod

Return Value: A Double specifying the present value of an annuity

Description: Calculates the present value of an annuity (either an investment or loan) based on a regular number of future payments of a fixed value and a fixed interest rate. The *present value* is the current value of a future stream of equal cash flows discounted at some fixed interest rate.

Rate Function   Microsoft.VisualBasic.Financial

```
Rate(nper, pmt, pv[, fv[, due[, guess]]])
```

nper   *required; Double*
   The total number of periods in the annuity.

pmt   *required; Double*
   The payment amount per period.

pv   *required; Double*
   The present value of the payments or future receipts.

fv   *optional; Double*
   The future value or cash balance after the final payment. If omitted, its value defaults to 0.

due   *optional;* DueDate *enumeration*
   A flag indicating whether payments are due at the beginning of the payment period (a value of DueDate.BegOfPeriod) or at the end of the payment period (a value of DueDate.EndOfPeriod, the default).

guess   *optional; Double*
   An estimate of the value to be returned by the function. If omitted, its value defaults to .1 (10%).

Return Value: A Double representing the interest rate per period

Description: Calculates the interest rate for an annuity (a loan or an investment) that consists of fixed payments over a known duration.

SLN Function   Microsoft.VisualBasic.Financial

```
SLN(cost, salvage, life)
```

cost   *required; Double*
   The initial cost of the asset

---

salvage   *required; Double*
    The value of the asset at the end of its useful life

life   *required; Double*
    The length of the useful life of the asset

Return Value: A Double representing depreciation per period

Description: Computes the straight-line depreciation of an asset for a single period

SYD Function
Microsoft.VisualBasic.Financial

SYD(*cost, salvage, life, period*)

cost   *required; Double*
    The initial cost of the asset

salvage   *required; Double*
    The value of the asset at the end of its useful life

life   *required; Double*
    The length of the useful life of the asset

period   *required; Double*
    The period whose depreciation is to be calculated

Return Value: A Double giving the sum-of-years depreciation of an asset for a given period

Description: Computes the sum-of-years' digits depreciation of an asset for a specified period. The sum-of-years' digits method allocates a larger amount of the depreciation in the earlier years of the asset.

Information

Erl Property

See "Erl Property" entry under "Error Handling" section.

IsArray Function

See "IsArray Function" entry under "Array Handling" section.

IsDate Function   Microsoft.VisualBasic.Information

IsDate(*expression*)

expression   *required; any*
    Expression containing a date or time

Return Value: Boolean indicating whether the expression can be converted to a Date

Description: Determines if an expression is of type Date or can be converted to type Date

Returns True if *expression* is of type Date or can be converted to type Date. Uninitialized date variables also return True.

IsDBNull Function   Microsoft.VisualBasic.Information

IsDBNull(*expression*)

expression   *required; any expression*
    Any value retrieved from or to be written to a database

Return Value: Boolean

Description: Determines whether *expression* evaluates to DbNull (that is, is equal to System.DbNull.Value).

IsError Function

See "IsError Function" entry under "Error Handling" section.

IsNothing Function   Microsoft.VisualBasic.Information

IsNothing(*expression*)

expression   *required; any*
    Any variable or expression to be tested for a null object reference

Return Value: Boolean

Description: Determines whether *expression* evaluates to Nothing. The line:

```
If IsNothing(obj) Then
```

is equivalent to:

```
If obj Is Nothing Then
```

IsNumeric Function

Microsoft.VisualBasic.Information

```
IsNumeric(expression)
```

expression   *required; any expression*
   An expression to be converted to a number

Return Value: Boolean

Description: Determines whether *expression* can be evaluated as a number. If the expression passed to *IsNumeric* evaluates to a number, True is returned; otherwise, *IsNumeric* returns False.

IsReference Function

Microsoft.VisualBasic.Information

```
IsReference(expression)
```

expression   *required; any*
   Any potential reference type

Return Value: Boolean

Description: Returns True if *expression* contains reference type data, as opposed to value type data.

RGB Function

See "RGB Function" entry under "Other Conversion" section.

Rem Statement

```
Rem comment
' comment
```

comment   *optional*
   A textual comment to place within the code

Description: Use the Rem statement or an apostrophe (') to place remarks within the code.

ScriptEngine Property
Microsoft.VisualBasic.Globals

ScriptEngine

Return Value: A String containing the value "VB"

Description: Indicates the programming language currently in use.

ScriptEngineBuildVersion Property
Microsoft.VisualBasic.Globals

ScriptEngineBuildVersion( )

Return Value: An Integer containing the build number

Description : Returns the build number of the VB.NET language engine.

ScriptEngineMajorVersion Property
Microsoft.VisualBasic.Globals

ScriptEngineMajorVersion

Return Value: An Integer containing the major version number

Description: Indicates the major version (1, 2, etc.) of the programming language currently in use.

ScriptEngineMinorVersion Property
Microsoft.VisualBasic.Globals

ScriptEngineMinorVersion

Return Value: An Integer containing the minor version number

Description: Indicates the minor version (the number to the right of the decimal point) of the programming language currently in use.

SystemTypeName Function
Microsoft.VisualBasic.Information

SystemTypeName(*vbname*)

vbname   *required; String*
    The name of a VB.NET data type

Return Value: A String indicating the name of a CTS data type

---

Description: Returns the fully qualified type name of the CTS data type that corresponds to a particular Visual Basic data type.

TypeName Function

Microsoft.VisualBasic.Information

TypeName(*varname*)

varname   *required; String literal*
    Name of a variable

Return Value: String

Description: Returns a string giving data type information about *varname*. The possible return values are:

String returned	Variable contents
Boolean	8-bit True or False value type
Byte	8-bit binary value type
Char	16-bit character value type
Date	64-bit date and time value type
DBNull	Reference type indicating missing or nonexistent data
Decimal	96-bit fixed point numeric value type
Double	64-bit floating point numeric value type
Error	Error object
Integer	32-bit integer value type
Long	64-bit integer value type
Nothing	Object variable with no object currently assigned to it, uninitialized string, or undimensioned array
Object	Reference type pointing to an unspecialized object
Short	16-bit integer value type
Single	32-bit floating point numeric value type
String	Reference type pointing to a string of 16-bit characters
<objectclass>	Reference type pointing to a specialized object created from class <objectclass>
<structure>	A variable created from a structure or user-defined type named structure
<typename>()	Dimensioned array

VarType Function
Microsoft.VisualBasic.Information

VarType(*varname*)

varname   *required; any*
    The name of a variable

Return Value: A member of the VariantType enumeration indicating the variable type

Description: Determines the data type of a variable.

VbTypeName Function
Microsoft.VisualBasic.Information

VbTypeName(*urtname*)

urtname   *required; String*
    The name of a CTS datatype

Return Value: A String containing the name of a VB.NET datatype

Description: Returns the name of the VB.NET datatype that corresponds to a particular CTS datatype.

Input/Output

EOF Function
Microsoft.VisualBasic.FileSystem

EOF(*filenumber*)

filenumber   *required; Integer*
    Any valid file number

Return Value: A Boolean indicating whether the end of the file has been reached

Description: Returns a Boolean indicating whether the end of the file has been reached. Applies to files opened for binary, random, or sequential input.

FileAttr Function
Microsoft.VisualBasic.FileSystem

FileAttr(*filenumber*)

filenumber   *required; Integer*
   Any valid file number

Return Value: An OpenMode constant, as shown in the following table:

Mode	Value
Input	1
Output	2
Random	4
Append	8
Binary	32

Description: Returns the file-access mode for a file opened using the *FileOpen* procedure

FileClose Procedure   Microsoft.VisualBasic.FileSystem

FileClose([*filenumber*][, *filenumber*][,...])

filenumber   *optional; Integer*
   The file number (or numbers) of file (or files) opened using the *FileOpen* procedure

Description: Closes one or more files opened with the *FileOpen* procedure

FileGet, FileGetObject Procedures   Microsoft.VisualBasic.FileSystem

FileGet(*FileNumber, Value, RecordNumber*)
FileGetObject(*FileNumber, Value, RecordNumber*)

FileNumber   *required; Integer*
   Any valid file number

Value   *required; any (object for FileGetObject)*
   Variable in which to place file contents

RecordNumber   *optional; Integer*
   The location at which reading begins

Description: Copies data from a file on disk into a variable.

FileLen Function

Microsoft.VisualBasic.FileSystem

`FileLen(pathname)`

pathname   *required; String*
> The filename, along with its path and drive name (optionally)

Return Value: A Long containing the length of the specified file in bytes

Description: Specifies the length of a file on disk.

FileOpen Procedure

Microsoft.VisualBasic.FileSystem

`FileOpen(filenumber, filename, mode, access, share, _`
`    recordlength)`

filenumber   *required; Integer*
> An available file number.

filename   *required; String*
> The name of the file to open, along with an optional path.

mode   *optional; OpenMode enum*
> The file-access mode. Options are: `OpenMode.Append`, `OpenMode.Binary`, `OpenMode.Input`, `OpenMode.Output`, or `OpenMode.Random` (the default value).

access   *optional; OpenAccess enum*
> Specifies the allowable operations by the current process. Options are: `OpenAccess.Default`, `OpenAccess.Read`, `OpenAccess.ReadWrite` (the default value), or `OpenAccess.Write`.

share   *optional; OpenShare enum*
> Specifies the allowable operations by other processes. Options are: `OpenShare.Shared` (the default value), `OpenShare.LockRead`, `OpenShare. LockWrite`, or `OpenShare.LockreadWrite`.

recordlength   *optional; Integer (at most, 32767)*
> The length of the record (for random access) or of the I/O buffer (for sequential access).

Description: Opens a disk file for reading and/or writing.

FilePut, FilePutObject Procedures   Microsoft.VisualBasic.FileSystem

```
FilePut(filenumber, value, [recordnumber])
FilePutObject(filenumber, value, [recordnumber])
```

filenumber   required; Integer
   Any valid file number

value   required; any (object for FilePutObject)
   The name of the variable containing the data to be written to
   the file

recordnumber   optional; Integer
   Record number (for random access) or byte number (for
   binary access) at which to begin the write operation

Description: Writes data from a program variable to a disk file.

FileWidth Procedure   Microsoft.VisualBasic.FileSystem

```
FileWidth(filenumber, recordwidth)
```

filenumber   required; Integer
   Any valid file number

recordwidth   required; Numeric
   A number between 0 and 255

Description: Specifies a virtual file width when working with files
opened with the *FileOpen* function.

FreeFile Function   Microsoft.VisualBasic.FileSystem

```
FreeFile()
```

Return Value: An integer representing the next available file
number

Description: Returns the next available file number for use in a
FileOpen function.

Input Procedure   Microsoft.VisualBasic.FileSystem

```
Input(filenumber, value)
```

filenumber   required; Integer
   Any valid file number

value   *required; any*
    Data to read from file

Description: Reads delimited data from a file into variables. This statement is used to read files that were created using the *Write* procedure, in which case the items are comma delimited with quotation marks around strings.

InputString Function   Microsoft.VisualBasic.FileSystem

InputString(*filenumber*, *charcount*)

filenumber   *required; Integer*
    Any valid file number

charcount   *required; Integer*
    Number of characters to read from file

Return Value: A String containing *charcount* characters

Description: Reads data from a file into a string variable.

LineInput Function   Microsoft.VisualBasic.FileSystem

LineInput(*filenumber*)

filenumber   *required; Integer*
    Any valid file number

Return Value: A String containing the line read from the file

Description: Assigns a single line from a sequential file opened in Input mode to a string variable.

Loc Function   Microsoft.VisualBasic.FileSystem

Loc(*filenumber*)

filenumber   *required; Integer*
    Any valid file number

Return Value: A Long indicating the current position of the read/write pointer in a file

Description: Determines the current position of the file read/write pointer.

Lock Procedure

```
Lock(filenumber[, record])            Syntax 1.
Lock(filenumber[, fromrecord,torecord]    Syntax 2.
```

filenumber   required; Integer
    Any valid file number

record   optional; Long
    The record or byte number at which to commence the lock

fromrecord   optional; Long
    The first record or byte number to lock

torecord   optional; Long
    The last record or byte number to lock

Description: The *Lock* procedure prevents another process from accessing a record, section, or whole file until it is unlocked by the *Unlock* function.

Use the *Lock* procedure in situations where multiple programs or more than one instance of your program may need read and write access to the same data file.

LOF Function

LOF(*filenumber*)

filenumber   required; Integer
    Any valid file number

Return Value: Long Integer

Description: Returns the size of an open file in bytes.

Print, PrintLine Procedures

```
Print(filenumber, [outputlist( )])
PrintLine(filenumber, [outputlist( )])
```

filenumber   required; Integer
    Any valid file number.

outputlist   optional; Parameter Array
    A comma-separated list of expressions to output to a file. *outputlist* can be either a scalar variable, a list of comma-

delimited expressions, or a parameter array. Its comma-delimited expressions or parameter array can include the following:

Spc(*n*)   *optional*
    Insert *n* space characters before expression.

Tab(*n*)   *optional*
    Position the insertion point either at the next print zone (by omitting *n*) or at column number (*n*).

expression   *optional; any*
    The data expression to output.

Description: Outputs formatted data to a disk file opened for Append or Output

---

Reset Procedure   Microsoft.VisualBasic.FileSystem

Reset( )

Description: Closes all files that have been opened using the *File-Open* procedure.

Seek Function   Microsoft.VisualBasic.FileSystem

Seek(*filenumber*)

filenumber   *required; Integer*
    Any valid file number

Return Value: A Long indicating the current read/write position

Description: Returns the current position of the read/write marker in the open file *filenumber*.

Seek Procedure   Microsoft.VisualBasic.FileSystem

Seek(*filenumber, position*)

filenumber   *required; Integer*
    Any valid file number

position   *required; Long*
    Any whole number between 1 and 2,147,483,647

Description: Places the read/write marker at a given position where the next read/write operation should occur.

Spc Function
Microsoft.VisualBasic.FileSystem

Spc(*n*)

n   *required; Integer*
    The number of spaces required

Return Value: A String containing *n* spaces

Description: Inserts spaces between expressions in a *Print* or *PrintLine* procedure.

Tab Function
Microsoft.VisualBasic.FileSystem

Tab[(*column*)]

column   *optional; Short*
    A column number to which the insertion point will move before displaying or printing the next expression

Return Value: A TabInfo structure

Description: Moves the text-insertion point to a given column or to the start of the next print zone.

IDE

#Region...#End Region Directive

```
#Region "identifier_string"
' code goes here
#End Region
```

identifier_string   *required; String literal*
    The title of the code block (or region)

Description: Marks a block of code as an expandable and collapsible region or code block in the Visual Studio .NET editor.

Interaction

AppActivate Procedure   Microsoft.VisualBasic.Interaction

[Interaction.]AppActivate(*title*)

title   *required; String or Integer*
> The name of the application as currently shown in the application window title bar. This can also be the task ID returned from the *Shell* function.

Description: Activates a window based on its caption.

Beep Procedure   Microsoft.VisualBasic.Interaction

Beep

Description: Sounds a tone through the computer's speaker.

Choose Function   Microsoft.VisualBasic.Interaction

Choose(*index*, *item_1*[,*item_2*, ...[, *item_n*]])

index   *required; Single*
> An expression that evaluates to the (1-based) index of the object to choose from the list

item_1-item_n   *required; any*
> A comma-delimited list of values from which to choose, or a ParamArray containing values from which to choose

Named Arguments: No

Return Value: The object chosen from the list

Description: Programmatically selects an object from a predefined list of objects (which are passed as parameters to the function) based on its ordinal position in the list. Using *Choose* is a simpler alternative to populating an array with fixed values.

Command Function   Microsoft.VisualBasic.Interaction

Command( )

Return Value: A String containing the command-line arguments

Description: Returns the command line arguments used when launching VB or an application created with VB.

Environ Function

Environ(*expression*)

expression   required; String, or a numeric expression
    If *expression* is a string, it must be the name of the required environment variable; if *expression* is numeric, it must be the 1-based ordinal number of the environment variable within the environment table.

Return Value: A String containing the text assigned to *expression*

Description: Returns the value assigned to an operating-system environment variable.

IIf Function

IIf(*expression, truepart, falsepart*)

expression   required; Boolean
    Expression to be evaluated

truepart   required; any value or expression
    Expression or value to return if *expression* is True

falsepart   required; any value or expression
    Expression or value to return if *expression* is False

Return Value: The value or result of the expression indicated by *truepart* or *falsepart*

Description: Returns one of two results, depending on whether *expression* evaluates to True or False. The function is typically avoided, particularly inside of a loop, because of its poor performance.

InputBox Function

InputBox(*prompt*[, *title*] [, *defaultresponse*] [, *xpos*] _
    [, *ypos*])

prompt   required; String
    The message in the dialog box

title   *optional; String*
    The title bar of the dialog box

defaultresponse   *optional; String*
    String to be displayed in the text box on loading

xpos   *optional; Numeric*
    The distance in twips from the left-hand side of the screen to
    the left-hand side of the dialog box

ypos   *optional; Numeric*
    The distance in twips from the top of the screen to the top of
    the dialog box

Return Value: A String containing the contents of the text box
from the *InputBox* dialog box

Description: Displays a dialog box containing a prompt for the
user, a text box for entering data, and an OK, a Cancel, and
(optionally) a Help button. When the user clicks OK, the function returns the contents of the text box.

MsgBox Function   Microsoft.VisualBasic.Interaction

MsgBox(*prompt*[, *buttons*][, *title*])

prompt   *required; String*
    The text of the message to display in the message box dialog
    box

buttons   *optional;* MsgBoxStyle *enumeration*
    The sum of the Button, Icon, Default Button, and Modality
    constant values

title   *optional; String*
    The title displayed in the title bar of the message box dialog
    box

Return Value: A MsgBoxResult enumeration constant indicating
the button clicked by the user to close the message box

Description: Displays a dialog box containing a message, buttons,
and optional icon to the user. The action taken by the user is
returned by the function in the form of an enumerated constant.

Partition Function \ Microsoft.VisualBasic.Interaction

Partition(*number*, *start*, *stop*, *interval*)

number   required; Long
  Number to evaluate against the intervals

start   required; Long
  Start of the range. Must be non-negative

stop   required; Long
  End of the range. Must be greater than *start*

interval   required; Long
  Size of each interval into which the range is partitioned

Return Value: A String containing the range within which *number* falls

Description: Returns a string that describes which interval contains the number.

Shell Function Microsoft.VisualBasic.Interaction

Shell(*pathname*[,*style*][, *Wait*][, *Timeout*])

pathname   required; String
  Name of the program to execute

style   optional; AppWinStyle *enumeration*
  The style of window and whether it receives the focus; its default value is AppWinStyle.MinimizedFocus.

Wait   optional; Boolean
  Boolean indicating whether to wait for the *pathname* application to finish execution before continuing execution of subsequent code; its default value is False.

Timeout   optional; Integer
  If *Wait* is True, number of milliseconds to wait for the *pathname* application to terminate before the *Shell* function times out. Its default value is -1 indicating that there is no timeout value.

Return Value: An Integer representing the Process ID, or 0

Description: Launches another application and, if successful, returns that application's task ID.

Switch Function   Microsoft.VisualBasic.Interaction

```
Switch(expr-1, value-1[, expr-2, value-2 ... [, _
    expr-n,value-n]]])
```

expr   *required; Object*
    A number of expressions to be evaluated

value   *required; Object*
    An expression or value to return if the associated expression
    evaluates to True

Return Value: An Object value or expression

Description: Evaluates a list of expressions and, on finding the
first expression to evaluate to True, returns an associated value or
expression.

If none of the expressions is True, the *Switch* function returns
Nothing.

If multiple expressions are True, *Switch* returns the value that
corresponds to the first True expression.

Mathematics

Abs Function   System.Math

```
Math.Abs(value)
```

value   *required; any valid numeric expression*
    A number whose absolute value is to be returned

Return Value: The absolute value of *value*. The data type is the
same as that of the argument passed to the function

Description: Returns the absolute value of *value*. If *value* is an
uninitialized variable, the return value is 0.

Acos Function   System.Math

```
Math.Acos(d)
```

d   *required; Double or any valid numeric expression*
A cosine, which is a number greater than or equal to −1 and less than or equal to 1

Return Value: A Double between 0 and pi that is the arccosine of *d* in radians

Description: Returns the arccosine of *d* in radians.

Asin Function   System.Math

```
Math.Asin(d)
```

d   *required; Double or any valid numeric expression*
A number representing a sine, which can range from −1 to 1

Return Value: A Double between −pi/2 and pi/2 that is the arcsine of *d* in radians

Description: Returns the arcsine of *d*, in radians

Atan Function   System.Math

```
Math.Atan(d)
```

d   *required; Double or any valid numeric expression*
A number representing a tangent

Return Value: A Double that is the arctangent in radians of *d*, in the range −pi/2 to pi/2

Description: Takes the ratio of two sides of a right triangle (*d*) and returns the corresponding angle in radians. The ratio is the length of the side opposite the angle divided by the length of the side adjacent to the angle.

Atan2 Function   System.Math

```
Math.Atan2(y, x)
```

x   *required; Double*
The x coordinate of a point

y   *required; Double*
The y coordinate of a point

Return Value: A Double that is the arctangent of the *ratio* x/y, in radians

Description: Returns the angle in the Cartesian plane formed by the x-axis and a vector starting from the origin (0,0) and terminating at the point (x, y). More specifically, the return value *q* satisfies the following:

- For (x, y) in quadrant 1, $0 < q < pi/2$
- For (x, y) in quadrant 2, $pi/2 < q < pi$
- For (x, y) in quadrant 3, $-pi < q < -pi/2$
- For (x, y) in quadrant 4, $-pi/2 < q < 0$

Ceiling Function   System.Math

`Math.Ceiling(a)`

a   *required; Double*
    Any valid numeric expression

Return Value: A Double containing the smallest integer greater than or equal to the argument *a*

Description: Returns the smallest integer greater than or equal to the argument *a*.

Cos Function   System.Math

`Math.Cos(d)`

d   *required; Double or numeric expression*
    An angle in radians

Return Value: A Double data type denoting the cosine of an angle

Description: Takes an angle specified in radians and returns a ratio representing the length of the side adjacent to the angle divided by the length of the hypotenuse.

Cosh Function   System.Math

`Math.Cosh(value)`

value   *required; Double or numeric expression*
    An angle in radians

Return Value: A Double denoting the hyperbolic cosine of the angle

Description: Returns the hyperbolic cosine of an angle.

E Field

System.Math

`Math.E`

Description: This field returns the approximate value of the irrational number e, which is the base of the natural logarithm and the base of the natural exponential function. In particular:

`Math.E = 2.71828182845905`

Exp Function

System.Math

`Math.Exp(d)`

d   *required; Numeric*
    Any valid numeric expression

Return Value: Double

Description: Returns a Double representing the natural number e raised to the power *d*. Note that the irrational number e is *approximately* 2.7182818.

Fix Function

See "Fix Function" entry under "Other Conversions" section.

Floor Function

System.Math

`Math.Floor(d)`

d   *required; Double*

Return Value: A Double containing the largest integer less than or equal to the argument *d*

Description: Returns the largest integer less than or equal to the argument *d*.

IEEERemainder Function   System.Math

`Math.IEEERemainder(x, y)`

x and y   *required; Double*

Return Value: Returns the remainder after dividing *x* by *y*

Description: Returns a Double whose value is the remainder after dividing *x* by *y*.

Int Function

See "Int Function" entry under "Other Conversions" section.

Log Function   System.Math

`Math.Log(d)`   *Syntax 1.*
`Math.Log(a, newbase)`   *Syntax 2.*

d or a   *required; Double*
   A numeric expression greater than zero

newbase   *required; Double*
   The base of the logarithm

Return Value: Double

Description: Returns the natural (base e) logarithm of a given number (the first syntax) or the logarithm of a given number in a specified base (the second syntax).

Log10 Function   System.Math

`Math.Log10(d)`

d   *required; Double*
   A numeric expression greater than zero

Return Value: Double

Description: Returns the common (base-10) logarithm of a given number.

Max Function
System.Math

`Math.Max(val1, val2)`

val1, val2   *required; any*
    A numeric data type or expression

Return Value: Returns the maximum of *val1* and *val2*, in the wider datatype of the two numbers

Description: Returns the maximum of *val1* and *val2*.

Min Function
System.Math

`Math.Min(val1, val2)`

val1, val2   *required; any numeric*
    A numeric data type or expression

Return Value: Returns the minimum of *val1* and *val2* in the wider data type of the two numbers

Description: Returns the minimum of two numbers.

Mod Operator

`result = number1 Mod number2`

number1, number2   *required; any*
    A numeric expression

Return Value: Returns the modulus

Description: Returns the modulus, that is, the remainder when *number1* is divided by *number2*. This return value is a non-negative integral data type.

Partition Statement

See "Partition Statement" entry under "Interaction" section.

Pi Field
System.Math

`Math.PI`

Return Value: A Double containing the approximate value of the irrational number pi

Description: This field returns the approximate value of the irrational number pi. In particular:

```
Math.PI = 3.14159265358979
```

Pow Function   System.Math

```
result = Math.Pow(x, y)
```

x, y   *required; Double*

Return Value: A Double that is *x* (the base) raised to the power *y* (the exponent)

Description: This is a generalized exponential function; it returns the result of a number raised to a specified power.

Randomize Procedure   Microsoft.VisualBasic.VBMath

```
Randomize([number])
```

number   *optional; Object or any valid numeric expression*
    A number used to initialize the random-number generator

Description: Initializes the random-number generator.

Rnd Function   Microsoft.VisualBasic.VBMath

```
Rnd[(number)]
```

number   *optional; Single*
    Any valid numeric expression that serves as a seed value

Return Value: A Single data type random number

Description: Returns a random number.

Round Function   System.Math

```
Math.Round( value[,digits])
```

value   *required; Numeric expression*
    Any numeric expression

digits   *optional; Integer*
      The number of places to include after the decimal point

Return Value: The same data type as *value*

Description: Rounds a given number to a specified number of decimal places.

Sign Function   System.Math

Sign(*value*)

value   *required; any numeric type, including Decimal*
      A numeric expression

Return Value: Integer

Description: Determines the sign of a number.

Sin Function   System.Math

Sin(*a*)

a   *required; Numeric*
      An angle expressed in radians

Return Value: A Double containing the sine of an angle

Description: Returns the ratio of two sides of a right triangle in the range −1 to 1.

Sinh Function   System.Math

Math.Sinh(*value*)

value   *required; Double or numeric expression*
      An angle in radians

Return Value: A Double denoting the hyperbolic sine of the angle

Description: Returns the hyperbolic sine of an angle.

Sqrt Function   System.Math

Sqr(*d*)

---

d   *required; Double*
    Any numeric expression greater than or equal to 0

Return Value: A Double containing the square root of *d*

Description: Calculates the square root of a given number.

Tan Function   System.Math

`Tan(a)`

a   *required; Double*
    An angle in radians

Return Value: A Double containing the tangent of an angle

Description: Returns the ratio of two sides of a right angle triangle.

Tanh Function   System.Math

`Math.Tanh(number)`

number   *required; Double or numeric expression*
    An angle in radians

Return Value: A Double denoting the hyperbolic tangent of the angle

Description: Returns the hyperbolic tangent of an angle.

Program Structure and Flow

Call Statement

`[Call] procedurename[(argumentlist)]`

procedurename   *required; n/a*
    The name of the subroutine being called

argumentlist   *optional; any*
    A comma-delimited list of arguments to pass to the subroutine being called

Description: Passes execution control to a procedure, function, or DLL procedure or function.

CallByName Function

CallByName(*Object, ProcName, UseCallType, Args( )*)

Object   *required; Object*

    A reference to the object containing the procedure being called.

ProcName   *required; String*

    The name of the procedure to call.

UseCallType   *required; CallType constant*

    A constant of type CallType indicating what type of procedure is being called. The CallType constants are:

Constant	Value	Description
Method	1	The called procedure is a method
Get	2	The called procedure retrieves a property value
Let	4	The called procedure sets the value of a property

Args   *optional; any*

    A ParamArray argument representing the arguments required by the procedure being called.

Named Arguments: Yes, if *Args*( ) is omitted

Return Value: Depends on the return value (if any) of the called procedure

Description: Provides a method for calling a class member by name.

Since *ProcName* is a string expression, rather than the literal name of a routine, it is possible to call routines dynamically at runtime using a string variable to hold the various procedure names.

Do...Loop Statement

```
Do [{While | Until} condition]      Syntax 1.
   [statements]
[Exit Do]
   [statements]
Loop
```

```
Do                          Syntax 2.
    [statements]
[Exit Do]
    [statements]
Loop [{While | Until} condition]
```

condition   *optional; Boolean expression*
    An expression that evaluates to True or False

statements   *optional*
    Program statements that are repeatedly executed while, or
    until, *condition* is True

Description: Repeatedly executes a block of code while or until a
condition becomes True.

End... Statement

```
End
End Class
End Enum
End Function
End Get
End If
End Interface
End Module
End Namespace
End Property
End Select
End Set
End Structure
End Sub
End SyncLock
End Try
End With
End While
```

Description: Ends a procedure or a block of code.

Exit... Statement

```
Exit Do
Exit For
Exit Function
Exit Property
```

```
Exit Select
Exit Sub
Exit Try
Exit While
```

Description: Prematurely exits a block of code.

For...Next Statement

```
For counter = initial_value To maximum_value _
            [Step stepcounter]
    'code to execute on each iteration
    [Exit For]
Next [counter]
```

counter   required (optional with Next statement);
                                           any valid numeric variable
    A variable that serves as the loop counter

initial_value   required; any valid numeric expression
    The starting value of *counter* for the first iteration of the loop

maximum_value   required; any valid numeric expression
    The value of *counter* during the last iteration of the loop

stepcounter   optional (required if Step is used);
                                       any valid numeric expression
    The amount by which *counter* is to be incremented or decremented on each iteration of the loop

Description: Defines a loop that executes a given number of times, as determined by a loop counter.

To use the For...Next loop, you must assign a numeric value to a counter variable. This counter is either incremented or decremented automatically with each iteration of the loop. In the For statement, you specify the value that is to be assigned to the counter initially and the maximum value the counter will reach for the block of code to be executed. The Next statement marks the end of the block of code that is to execute repeatedly, and it also serves as a kind of flag that indicates that the counter variable is to be modified.

For Each...Next Statement

```
For Each element In group
[statements]
[Exit For]
[statements]
Next [element]
```

element   *required; Object or any user-defined object type*
An object variable to which the current element from the group is assigned

group   *required*
An object collection or array

statements   *optional*
A line or lines of program code to execute within the loop

Description: Loops through the items of a collection or the elements of an array.

GoTo Statement

```
GoTo label
```

label   *required; string literal*
A subroutine name

Description: Passes execution to a specified line within a procedure.

If...Then...Else Statement

Standard syntax:
```
If condition Then
    [statements]
[ElseIf condition-n Then
    [elseifstatements] ...
[Else
    [elsestatements]]
End If
```
One-line syntax:
```
If condition Then [statements] [Else elsestatements]
```

condition   *required; Boolean*
An expression returning either True or False or an object type

---

statements   *optional*
    Program code to be executed if *condition* is true

condition-n   *optional*
    Same as condition

elseifstatements   *optional*
    Program code to be executed if the corresponding *condition-n* is True

elsestatements   *optional*
    Program code to be executed if the corresponding *condition* or *condition-n* is False

Description: Executes a statement or block of statements based on the Boolean (True or False) value of an expression.

Return Statement

```
Return              In a subroutine
Return ReturnValue  In a function
```

ReturnValue   *required; any*
    The return value of the function

Description: Returns to the calling program from a subroutine or function.

Select Case Statement

```
Select Case testexpression
   [Case expressionlist-n
      [statements-n]] ...
   [Case Else
      [elsestatements]]
End Select
```

testexpression   *required; any*
    Any numeric or string expression whose value determines which block of code is executed.

expressionlist-n   *required; any*
    Comma-delimited list of expressions to compare values with *testexpression*

---

statements-n *optional*
> Program statements to execute if a match is found between any section of *expressionlist* and *testexpression*

elsestatements *optional*
> Program statements to execute if a match between *testexpression* and any *expressionlist* cannot be found

expressionlist can use any (or a combination of any) of the following:

expressionlist syntax	Examples
expression	`iVar - iAnotherVar` `iVar`

expression To *expression*	`5 To 10`
	`8 To 11, 13 to 15`
	`"A" To "D"`

Is *comparisonoperator expression*	`Is = 10`

Description: Allows for conditional execution of a block of code, typically out of three or more code blocks, based on some condition. Use the Select Case statement as an alternative to complex nested If...Then...Else statements.

Stop Statement

Stop

Description: Suspends program execution.

While...End While Statement

```
While condition
   [statements]
[Exit While]
   [statements]
End While
```

condition *required; Numeric or String*
> An expression evaluating to True or False

statements *optional*
> Program statements to execute while condition remains True

Exit While   *optional; Keyword*
    Exits the While loop

Description: Repeatedly executes program code while a given condition remains `True`.

Programming

AddHandler Statement

AddHandler *NameOfEventSender*, AddressOf *NameOfEventHandler*

NameOfEventSender   *required; String literal*
    The name of a class or object instance and its event, such as Button1.Click

NameOfEventHandler   *required; String literal*
    The name of a subroutine that is to serve as the event handler for *NameOfEventSender*

Description: Binds an event handler to a built in or custom event. This makes it possible to bind several event handlers to a single event.

- NameOfEventSender takes the form `class.event` or `object.event`
- You can stop handling events defined by the `AddHandler` statement by calling the `RemoveHandler` statement

AddressOf Operator

AddressOf *procedurename*

procedurename   *required*
    The name of a procedure that is referenced by the procedure delegate

Description: The `AddressOf` operator returns a procedure delegate instance that references a specific procedure. It is used in the following situations:

- If a parameter to a procedure (a VB procedure or a Win32 API function) requires a function pointer (the address of a function), then we can pass the expression:

```
AddressOf functionname
```

where *functionname* is the name of the function. This function is called a *callback function*.

- AddressOf is also used to create delegate objects, as in:

```
delg = New ADelegate(AddressOf obj.AMethod)
```

- AddressOf is used to bind event handlers to events through the AddHandler statement:

```
AddHandler Form1.Click, AddressOf Me.Form1Click
```

Class...End Class Statement

See "Class...End Class Statement" entry under "Declaration" section.

COMClass Attribute   Microsoft.VisualBasic.COMClassAttribute

Description: Adds metadata that allows a .NET class to be exposed as a COM object. You can supply the attribute with a class identifier, an interface identifier, and an event identifier. All are globally unique identifiers (GUIDs) that can be generated either by using the *guidgen.exe* utility or automatically by using the COM Class Wizard. They ensure that the COM component retains the same GUIDs when it is recompiled.

Constructor: New([[[*classID*], *interfaceID*], *eventID*])

classID   *String*
    The class identifier (CLSID) that will uniquely identify the COM class

interfaceID   *String*
    The interface identifier (IID) that uniquely identifies the class' default COM interface

eventID   *String*
    The event identifier that uniquely identifies an event

Properties

ClassID   *String*
    Read-only. Provides the CLSID that uniquely identifies a COM class. Its value is set by the *classID* parameter of the class constructor.

EventID   *String*

Read-only. Provides the GUID that uniquely identifies an event. Its value is set by the *eventID* parameter of the class constructor.

InterfaceID   *String*

Read-only. Provides the IID that uniquely identifies a COM interface. Its value is set by the *interfaceID* parameter of the class constructor.

InterfaceShadows   *Boolean*

Indicates whether the COM interface name is the same as the name of another member of the class or the base class. Its default value is False.

CreateObject Function   Microsoft.VisualBasic.Interaction

objectvariable = CreateObject(*progid* [, *servername*])

objectvariable   *required; Object*

A variable to hold the reference to the instantiated object

progid   *required; String*

The programmatic identifier (or ProgID) of the class of the object to create

servername   *optional; String*

The name of the server on which the object resides

Named Arguments: No

Return Value: A reference to a COM or ActiveX object

Description: Creates an instance of an OLE Automation (ActiveX) object.

Prior to calling the methods, functions, or properties of a COM or ActiveX object, you are required to create an instance of that object. Once an object is created, reference it in code using the object variable you defined.

Declare Statement

See "Declare Statement" entry under "Declaration" section.

Event Statement

```
[accessmodifier] [Shadows] Event eventName [(arglist)]
    [Implements interfacename.interfaceeventname]
```

accessmodifier   *optional; Keyword*
    Can be one of Public, Private, Protected, Friend, and
    Protected Friend.

Shadows   *optional; Keyword*
    Indicates that the event shadows any programming elements
    of the same name in a base class.

eventName   *required; String literal*
    The name of the event.

arglist is optional and has the following syntax:

```
[ByVal | ByRef] varname[( )] [As type]
```

ByVal   *optional; Keyword*
    The argument is passed by value; that is, a local copy of the
    variable is assigned the value of the argument. ByVal is the
    default method of passing variables.

ByRef   *optional; Keyword*
    The argument is passed by reference; that is, the local vari-
    able is simply a reference to the argument being passed. All
    changes made to the local variable are reflected in the calling
    argument.

varname   *required; String literal*
    The name of the local variable containing either the reference
    or value of the argument.

type   *optional; Keyword*
    The data type of the argument. It can be Byte, Boolean, Char,
    Short, Integer, Long, Single, Double, Decimal, Date, String,
    Object, or any user-defined structure, object type, or data
    type defined in the BCL.

Implements *interfacename.interfaceeventname*   *optional*
    Indicates that the event implements a particular event named
    interfaceeventname in the interface named *interfacename*.

Description: Defines a custom event that the object can raise at
any time using the RaiseEvent statement.

Environ Function

See "Environ Function" entry under "Interaction" section.

Get Statement

```
Get( )
   [ statements ]
End Get
```

statements   *optional*
    Program code to be executed when the Property Get proce-
    dure is called

Description: Defines a Property Get procedure that returns a
property value to the caller.

GetObject Function   Microsoft.VisualBasic.Interaction

GetObject([*pathname*] [, *class*])

pathname   *optional; String*
    The full path and name of the file containing the COM (or
    ActiveX) object.

class   *optional; String*
    The class of the object. The *class* argument has these parts:

Appname   *required; String*
    The name of the application.

Objecttype   *required; String*
    The class of object to create, delimited from *Appname* by
    using a period (.). For example, Appname.Objecttype.

Return Value: A reference to an ActiveX object

Description: Accesses an ActiveX server held within a specified
file.

Handles Keyword

```
Handles name.event
```

name   *required; String literal*
> The name of the class or object whose event the subroutine is handling

event   *required; String literal*
> The name of the event that the subroutine is handling

Description: Defines a procedure as the event handler for a particular event.

Implements Keyword

```
Implements interfacename.interfacemember [, ...]
```

interfacename   *required; String literal*
> The name of the interface being implemented by a class

interfacemember   *required; String literal*
> The name of the interface property, function, procedure, or event that is being implemented by a class

Description: Indicates that a class member provides the implementation of a member defined in an interface.

Implements Statement

```
Implements InterfaceName [,InterfaceName][,...]
```

InterfaceName   *required; String literal*
> The name of the interface that a class implements

Description: The Implements statement specifies that you will *implement* an interface within the class in which the Implements statement appears.

Imports Statement

```
Imports [aliasname = ] namespace [.element]
```

aliasname   *optional; String literal*
> The name by which the namespace will be referenced in the module

---

namespace   *required; String literal*
    The name of the namespace being imported

element   *optional*
    The name of an element in the namespace

Description: Imports namespaces or parts of namespaces, making their members available to the current module.

Inherits Statement

Inherits *classname*

classname   *required; String literal*
    The name of the inherited (base) class

Description: Specifies the name of the class that is being inherited, that is, the base class. The statement can appear immediately after the Class statement or the Interface statement.

Interface Statement

[*accessmodifier*] [Shadows] Interface *name*
...statements
End Interface

accessmodifier   *optional; Keyword*
    One of the following keywords, which determines the visibility of the interface:

    Public   *optional; Keyword*
        Indicates that the interface is publicly accessible anywhere both inside and outside of the project.

    Private   *optional; Keyword*
        Indicates that the interface is accessible to any nested types, as well as to the type (if any) in which it is defined.

    Protected   *optional; Keyword*
        Indicates that the interface is accessible only to derived classes; a protected interface can only be declared inside of a class.

    Friend   *optional; Keyword*
        Indicates that the interface is accessible only within the project that contains the interface definition.

Protected Friend   *optional; Keyword*
>   Indicates that the interface is declared inside of a class
>   and that it is accessible throughout the project that
>   contains the interface definition, as well as to derived
>   classes.

Shadows   *optional; Keyword*
>   Indicates that the interface shadows an identically named
>   element in a base class.

name   *required; String literal*
>   The name of the interface.

statements   *required*
>   Code that defines the interface members that derived classes
>   must implement.

Description: Defines a virtual base class along with its public
members. The interface can then be implemented by derived
classes using the Implements statement.

Is Operator

object1 Is *object2*

object1   *required; Object or any reference type*

object2   *required; Object or any reference type*

Return Value: Boolean

Description: Compares two object variables or reference variables
to determine whether they reference the same object.

Len Function   Microsoft.VisualBasic.Strings

Len(*expression*)

expression   *required; any*
>   Any valid variable name or expression

Return Value: Integer

Description: Counts the number of characters within a string or
the size of a given variable.

Me Operator

Me

Description: Represents a reference to the current class from within the class.

MyBase Keyword

MyBase

Description: Provides a reference to the base class from within a derived class. If you want to call a member of the base class from within a derived class, you can use the syntax:

    MyBase.*MemberName*

where *MemberName* is the name of the member. This will resolve any ambiguity if the derived class also has a member of the same name.

MyClass Keyword

MyClass

Description: Provides a reference to the class in which the keyword is used.

Namespace Statement

    Namespace *name*
        component types
    End Namespace

name   *required; String literal*
    The name of the namespace

component types   *required*
    The elements that are being declared as part of the namespace, including Enums, Structures, Interfaces, Classes, Delegates, Modules, and other namespaces

Description: Declares a namespace and specifies the items in it.

Property Statement

See "Property Statement" entry under "Declaration" section.

RaiseEvent Statement

```
RaiseEvent eventName([arglist])
```

eventName   *required; String literal*
    The name of the event

arglist   *optional; any (defined by the* Event *statement)*
    A comma-delimited list of arguments

Description: Generates a predefined, custom event within any procedure of an object module

RemoveHandler Statement

```
RemoveHandler NameOfEventSender, AddressOf NameOfEventHandler
```

NameOfEventSender   *required; String literal*
    The name of a class or object instance and its event, such as
    Button1.Click

NameOfEventHandler   *required; String literal*
    The name of a subroutine to remove as event handler for
    NameOfEventSender

Description: Removes a previous binding of an event handler to a built-in or custom event.

Shadows Keyword

```
Shadows
```

Description: When a member of a derived class has the same name as a member of the same type in the base class, and the keywords Overridable and Overrides are used appropriately, then the derived class member overrides the base class member. That is, any reference to the member using a derived class object refers to the implementation in the derived class.

Shadowing works in a similar way but allows any member type to "override" any other member type. Thus, for example, a method can "override" a property.

SyncLock Statement

```
SyncLock expression
...[ code ]
End SyncLock
```

expression   *required; any reference type (class, module, interface, array, or delegate)*
An expression yielding a single result that can be used to determine the accessibility of *code*

code   *optional*
The code statements to which access is synchronized and that will be executed sequentially

Description: Prevents multiple threads of execution in the same process from accessing shared data or resources at the same time

WithEvents Keyword

```
Dim|Private|Public WithEvents objVarName As objectType
```

objVarName   *required; String*
The name of any object variable that refers to an object that exposes events

objectType   *required; any object type other than the generic Object*
The ProgID of a referenced object

Description: Informs VB that the object being referenced exposes events for which you intend to provide event handlers.

Registry

DeleteSetting Procedure   Microsoft.VisualBasic.Interaction

```
DeleteSetting(appname[, section[, key]])
```

appname   *required; String*
> The name of the application. This must be a subkey of the
> HKEY_CURRENT_USER\Software\VB and VBA Program Settings
> registry key.

section   *optional; String*
> The name of the application key's subkey that is to be
> deleted. *section* can be a single key or a registry path sepa-
> rated with backslashes.

key   *optional; String*
> The name of the value entry to delete.

Description: Deletes a complete application key, one of its
subkeys, or a single value entry from the Windows registry.

GetAllSettings Function   Microsoft.VisualBasic.Interaction

GetAllSettings(*appname*, *section*)

appname   *required; String*
> Name of the application

section   *required; String*
> Relative path from *appname* to the key containing the settings
> to retrieve

Return Value: An object containing a two-dimensional array of
strings

Description: Returns the registry value entries and their corresponding values for the application.

GetSetting Function   Microsoft.VisualBasic.Interaction

GetSetting(*appname*, *section*, *key*[, *default*])

appname   *required; String*
> The name of the application

section   *required; String*
> The path from the application key to the key containing the
> value entries

key   *required; String*
> The name of the value entry whose value is to be returned

---

default   *optional; String*
    The value to return if no value can be found

Return Value: A string containing the value of the specified *key*; *default* if *key*, *section*, or *appname* were not found.

Description: Returns a single value from a specified section of your application's entry in the HKEY_CURRENT_USER\Software\VB and VBA Program Settings\ branch of the registry.

SaveSetting Procedure   Microsoft.VisualBasic.Interaction

SaveSetting(*appname*, *section*, *key*, *setting*)

appname   *required; String*
    The name of the application

section   *required; String*
    The name of the registry key

key   *required; String*
    The name of the value entry whose value is to be saved

setting   *required; String or numeric*
    The value to save

Description: Creates or saves an entry for a VB application in the Windows registry.

String Manipulation

Asc, AscW Functions   Microsoft.VisualBasic.Strings

Asc(*string*)
AscW(*str*)

string, str   *required; String or Char*
    Any expression that evaluates to a *nonempty* string

Return Value: An Integer that represents the character code of the first character of the string; the range for the returned value is 0 – 255 on nonDBCS systems, and –32768 to 32767 on DBCS systems

---

Description: Returns an Integer representing the character code for the first character of the string passed to it. All other characters in the string are ignored.

Chr, ChrW Functions   Microsoft.VisualBasic.Strings

```
Chr(charcode)
ChrW(charcode)
```

charcode   *required; Integer*
   An expression that evaluates to a Unicode character code

Return Value: A Char that contains the character represented by *charcode*

Description: Returns the character represented by the *charcode*.

Filter Function   Microsoft.VisualBasic.Strings

```
Filter(Source, Match[, Include[, Compare]])
```

Source   *required; String or Object*
   An array containing values to be filtered.

Match   *required; String*
   The substring of characters to find in the elements of the source array.

Include   *optional; Boolean*
   A Boolean (True or False) value. If True (the default value), *Filter* includes all matching values in the returned array; if False, *Filter* excludes all matching values (or, to put it another way, includes all nonmatching values).

Compare   *optional; CompareMethod enumeration*
   A constant whose value can be CompareMethod.Text or CompareMethod.Binary (the default).

Return Value: A 0-based String array of the elements filtered from *Source*

Description: The *Filter* function produces an array of matching values from an array of source values that either match or do not match a given filter string. Put another way, individual elements are copied from a source array to a target array if they either

---

match (*Include* is True) or do not match (*Include* is False) a filter string. A match occurs for an array element if *Match* is a substring of the array element.

Format Function

```
Format(expression[, style[, dayofweek[,  weekofyear]]])
```

expression   required; String/Numeric
    Any valid string or numeric expression

style   optional; String
    A valid named or user-defined format expression

dayofweek   optional; FirstDayOfWeek *enumeration*
    A constant that specifies the first day of the week, as shown in
    the following table:

Constant	Value	Description
System	0	NLS API setting
Sunday	1	Sunday (default)
Monday	2	Monday
Tuesday	3	Tuesday
Wednesday	4	Wednesday
Thursday	5	Thursday
Friday	6	Friday
Saturday	7	Saturday

weekofyear   optional; FirstWeekOfYear *enumeration*
    A constant that specifies the first week of the year, as shown
    in the following table:

First Week of Year Constants

Constant	Value	Description
UseSystemDayOfWeek	0	Use the NLS API setting
FirstJan1	1	Start with the week in which January 1 occurs (default)

Constant	Value	Description
FirstFourDays	2	Start with the first week that has at least four days in the new year
FirstFullWeek	3	Start with first full week of the year

Return Value: A string containing the formatted expression

Description: Allows you to use either predefined or user-defined formats to output string, numeric, and date/time data.

FormatCurrency, FormatNumber, FormatPercent Functions

Microsoft.VisualBasic.Strings

```
FormatCurrency(expression[,NumDigitsAfterDecimal][, _
    IncludeLeadingDigit[,UseParensForNegativeNumbers[, _
    GroupDigits]]]])
FormatNumber(expression[,NumDigitsAfterDecimal][, _
    IncludeLeadingDigit[,UseParensForNegativeNumbers[, _
    GroupDigits]]]])
FormatPercent(expression[,NumDigitsAfterDecimal][, _
    IncludeLeadingDigit[,UseParensForNegativeNumbers[, _
    GroupDigits]]]])
```

expression　　　　　　　　　　　　　　　*required; Object*
　　The number or numeric expression to be formatted.

NumDigitsAfterDecimal　　　　　　　　　　*optional; Long*
　　The number of digits the formatted string should contain after the decimal point.

IncludeLeadingDigit　　　　　*optional;* TriState *constant*
　　Indicates whether the formatted string is to have a 0 before floating point numbers between 1 and –1.

UseParensForNegativeNumbers　　*optional;* TriState *constant*
　　Specifies whether parentheses should be placed around negative numbers.

GroupDigits　　　　　　　　　*optional;* TriState *constant*
　　Determines whether digits in the returned string should be grouped using the delimiter specified in the computer's regional settings. For example, on English language systems, the value 1000000 is returned as 1,000,000 if *GroupDigits* is True.

Return Value: String

Description: Functions used to format currency, numbers, and percentages. The three functions are almost identical. They all take identical arguments. The only difference is that *FormatCurrency* returns a formatted number beginning with the currency symbol specified in the computer's regional settings, *FormatNumber* returns just the formatted number, and *FormatPercent* returns the formatted number followed by a percentage sign (%).

FormatDateTime Function

Microsoft.VisualBasic.Strings

```
FormatDateTime(expression[,dateformat])
```

expression   *required; Date*
    Date variable or literal date

dateformat   *optional;* DateFormat *enum*
    Defines the format of the date to return

Return Value: String representing the formatted date or time

Description: Formats a date or time expression based on the computer's regional settings.

GetChar Function

Microsoft.VisualBasic.Strings

```
GetChar(str, index)
```

str   *required; String*
    The string from which to extract a character

index   *required; Integer*
    Position of character (1-based)

Return Value: A Char containing the character at position *index*

Description: Returns the character that is at position *index* within a given string.

InStr Function

Microsoft.VisualBasic.Strings

```
InStr(start, string1, string2[, compare])     Syntax 1.
InStr(string1, string2[, compare])            Syntax 2.
```

---

start   *required in first syntax; Numeric*
    The starting position for the search

string1   *required; String*
    The string being searched

string2   *required; String*
    The string being sought

compare   *optional;* CompareMethod *enumeration*
    The type of string comparison

Return Value: An Integer indicating the position of the first occurrence of *string2* in *string1*

Description: Finds the starting position of one string within another.

InStrRev Function   Microsoft.VisualBasic.Strings

InstrRev(*stringcheck, stringmatch*[, *start*[, *compare*]])

stringcheck   *required; String*
    The string to be searched.

stringmatch   *required; String*
    The substring to be found within *stringcheck*.

start   *optional; Numeric*
    The starting position of the search. If no value is specified, *start* defaults to 1.

compare   *optional;* CompareMethod *enumeration*
    A constant indicating how *stringcheck* and *stringmatch* should be compared.

Return Value: Long

Description: Determines the starting position of a substring within a string by searching from the end of the string to its beginning.

Join Function

See "Join Function" entry under "Array Handling" section.

LCase Function

LCase(*value*)

value   *required; String or Char*
   A valid string expression or a character

Return Value: String or Char

Description: Converts a string to lowercase.

Left Function

Left(*str, length*)

str   *required; String*
   The string to be processed

length   *required; Long*
   The number of characters to return from the left of the string

Return Value: String

Description: Returns a string containing the leftmost *length* characters of *str*.

Len Function

See "Len Function" entry under "Programming" section.

Like Operator

result = *string* Like *pattern*

string   *required; String*
   The string to be tested against *pattern*

pattern   *required; String*
   A series of characters used by the Like operator to determine if *string* and *pattern* match

Return Type: Boolean

Description: If *string* matches *pattern*, *result* is True; otherwise, *result* is False.

LSet Function   Microsoft.VisualBasic.Strings

`LSet(Source, Length)`

Source   *required; String*
    The string to be left aligned

Length   *required; Integer*
    The length of the returned string

Return Value: String

Description: Left aligns a string.

LTrim Function   Microsoft.VisualBasic.Strings

`LTrim(str)`

str   *required; String*
    A valid string expression

Return Value: String

Description: Removes any leading spaces from *str*.

Mid Function   Microsoft.VisualBasic.Strings

`Mid(str, start[, length])`

str   *required; String*
    The expression from which to return a substring

start   *required; Long*
    The starting position of the substring

length   *optional; Long*
    The length of the substring

Return Value: String

Description: Returns a substring of a specified length from a given string.

Mid Statement

`Mid(target, start[, length]) = string`

---

target   required; *String*
    The name of the string variable to be modified

start   required; *Long*
    The position within *target* at which the replacement commences

length   optional; *Long*
    The number of characters in *target* to replace

string   required; *String*
    The string used to replace characters within *target*

Description: Replaces a section of a string with characters from another string.

Option Compare Statement

```
Option Compare {Binary | Text}
```

Description: Used to set the default method for comparing string data. Binary provides for a case sensitive comparison; text provides for a case insensitive comparison in which sort of order is based on the local system's locale settings

Replace Function   Microsoft.VisualBasic.Strings

```
Replace(expression, find, replace [, start[, _
     count[, compare]]])
```

expression   required; *String*
    The complete string containing the substring to be replaced

find   required; *String*
    The substring to be found by the function

replace   required; *String*
    The new substring to replace *find* in *expression*

start   optional; *Long*
    The character position in *expression* at which the search for *find* begins

count   optional; *Long*
    The number of instances of *find* to replace

compare   *optional;* CompareMethod *constant*
    The method used to compare *find* with *expression*; its value
    can be CompareMethod.Binary (for case-sensitive comparison)
    or CompareMethod.Text (for case-insensitive comparison)

Return Value: The return value from *Replace* depends on the
parameters you specify in the argument list, as the following table
shows:

If	Return value
expression = ""	Zero-length string ("")
find = ""	Copy of *expression*
replace = ""	Copy of *expression* with all instances of *find* removed
start > Len(*expression*)	Zero-length string ("")
count = 0	Copy of *expression*

Description: Replaces a given number of instances of a specified
substring in another string.

Right Function   Microsoft.VisualBasic.Strings

Right(*string, length*)

string   *required; String*
    The string to be processed

length   *required; Integer*
    The number of characters to return from the right of the string

Return Value: String

Description: Returns a string containing the rightmost *length*
characters of *string*.

RSet Function   Microsoft.VisualBasic.Strings

RSet(*Source, Length*)

Source   *required; String*
    The string to be right aligned

Length   *required; Integer*
> The length of the returned string

Return Value: String

Description: Right aligns a string.

RTrim Function   Microsoft.VisualBasic.Strings

RTrim(*string*)

string   *required; String*
> A valid string expression

Return Value: String

Description: Removes any trailing spaces from *string*.

Str Function

See "Str Function" entry under "Data Type Conversion" section.

Spc Function

See "Spc Function" entry under "Input/Output" section.

Space Function   Microsoft.VisualBasic.Strings

Space(*number*)

number   *required; Integer*
> An expression evaluating to the number of spaces required

Return Value: A String containing *number* spaces

Description: Creates a string containing *number* spaces.

Split Function   Microsoft.VisualBasic.Strings

Split(*expression*, [*delimiter*[, *limit*[, *compare*]]])

expression   *required; String*
> A string to be broken up into multiple strings.

delimiter   *optional; String*
> The character used to delimit the substrings in *expression*.

limit   *optional; Integer*
> The maximum number of strings to return.

compare   *optional;* CompareMethod *Constant*
> The method of comparison. Possible values are CompareMethod.Binary (the default) or CompareMethod.Text.

Return Value: A String array containing the substrings of *expression* delimited by *delimiter*

Description: Parses a single string containing delimited values into an array.

StrComp Function   Microsoft.VisualBasic.Strings

StrComp(*string1*, *string2*[, *compare*])

string1   *required; String*
> Any string expression

string2   *required; String*
> Any string expression

compare   *optional;* CompareMethod *constant*
> Either CompareMethod.Binary or CompareMethod.Text

Return Value: Integer

Description: Determines whether two strings are equal and, if not, which of two strings has the greater value.

StrConv Function   Microsoft.VisualBasic.Strings

StrConv(*str*, *conversion*[, *localeID*])

str   *required; String*
> The string expression to convert

conversion   *required; Constant of the* VbStrConv *enumeration*
> Constant specifying the type of string conversion.

localeID   *optional; Integer*
> The locale identifier to use for the conversion

Return Value: A String converted according to *conversion*

Description: Performs special conversions on a string.

StrDup Function   Microsoft.VisualBasic.Strings

StrDup(*number*, *character*)

number   required; Integer
    The number of times to duplicate the first character in string

character   required; String, Char, or Object
                                          containing a String or Char
    The String or Char whose first character is to be duplicated

Return Value: A String containing the character duplicated the specified number of times

Description: Returns a string that consists of the first character of *character* duplicated *number* times.

StrReverse Function   Microsoft.VisualBasic.Strings

StrReverse(*expression*)

expression   required; String
    The string whose characters are to be reversed

Return Value: String

Description: Returns a string that is the reverse of the string passed to it. For example, if the string and is passed to it as an argument, *StrReverse* returns the string dna.

Trim Function   Microsoft.VisualBasic.Strings

Trim(*str*)

str   required; String
    Any string expression

Return Value: String

Description: Removes both leading and trailing spaces from a given string.

UCase Function
Microsoft.VisualBasic.Strings

UCase(*value*)

value   *required; String*
    A valid string expression

Return Value: String

Description: Converts a string to uppercase.

Val Function

See "Val Function" entry under "Data Type Conversion" section.

VBFixedString Attribute
Microsoft.VisualBasic.VBFixedStringAttribute

Applies to: Field

Description: Defines a fixed-length string. It is the rough equivalent of the VB 6 declaration:

```
Dim s As String * length
```

It can be used to define fixed-length strings within structures, particularly structures that are to be passed to Win32 API functions, as well as to define fixed-length strings to be written to and read from random access files.

Constructor: New(*length*)

length   *Integer*
    The length of the string

Properties: *Length*   *Integer*
    Read-only. The length of the string. Its value is set by the *length* parameter in the class constructor.

Other Titles Available from O'Reilly

Microsoft .NET Programming

VB.NET Language in a Nutshell, 2nd Edition

By Steven Roman, Ron Petrusha & Paul Lomax
2nd Edition May 2002
682 pages, ISBN 0-596-00308-0

The documentation that comes with VB typically provides only the bare details for each language element; left out is the valuable inside information that a programmer really needs to know in order to solve programming problems or to use a particular language element effectively. *VB .NET Language in a Nutshell*, 2nd Edition documents the undocumented and presents the kind of wisdom that comes from the authors' many years of experience with the language. Bonus CD ingegrates the book's reference section with Visual Studio .NET.

Learning Visual Basic .NET

By Jesse Liberty
1st edition October 2002
320 pages, ISBN 0-596-00386-2

Learning Visual Basic .NET is a complete introduction to VB.NET and object-oriented programming. By using hundreds of examples, this book demonstrates how to develop various kinds of applications—including those that work with databases—and web services. *Learning Visual Basic .NET* will help you build a solid foundation in .NET.

Programming C#, 2nd Edition

By Jesse Liberty
2nd Edition February 2002
650 pages, ISBN 0-596-00309-9

The first part of *Programming C#*, 2nd Edition introduces C# fundamentals, then goes on to explain the development of desktop and Internet applications, including Windows Forms, ADO.NET, ASP.NET (including Web Forms), and Web Services. Next, this book gets to the heart of the .NET Framework, focusing on attributes and reflection, remoting, threads and synchronization, streams, and finally, it illustrates how to interoperate with COM objects.

Programming ASP.NET

By Jesse Liberty & Dan Hurwitz
1st Edition February 2002
960 pages, ISBN 0-596-00171-1

The ASP.NET technologies are so complete and flexible; your main difficulty may lie simply in weaving the pieces together for maximum efficiency.
Programming ASP.NET shows you how to do just that. Jesse Liberty and Dan Hurwitz teach everything you need to know to write web applications and web services using both C# and Visual Basic .NET.

O'REILLY®

C# in a Nutshell

By Peter Drayton & Ben Albarhari
1st Edition March 2002
856 pages, ISBN 0-596-00181-9

C# is likely to become one of the most widely used languages for building .NET applications. *C# in a Nutshell* contains a concise introduction to the language and its syntax, plus brief tutorials used to accomplish common programming tasks. It also includes O'Reilly's classic-style, quick-reference material for all the types and members in core .NET namespaces, including System, System.Text, System.IO, and System.Collections.

ASP.NET in a Nutshell

By G. Andrew Duthie &
Matthew MacDonald
1st Edition June 2002
816 pages, ISBN 0-596-00116-9

As a quick reference and tutorial in one, *ASP.NET in a Nutshell* goes beyond the published documentation to highlight little-known details, stress practical uses for particular features, and provide real-world examples that show how features can be used in a working application. This book covers application and web service development, custom controls, data access, security, deployment, and error handling. There is also an overview of web-related class libraries.

.NET Framework Essentials, 2nd Edition

By Thuan L. Thai, Hoang Lam
2nd Edition February 2002
320 pages, 0-596-00302-1

.NET Framework Essentials, 2nd Edition is a concise and technical overview of the Microsoft .NET Framework. Covered here are all of the most important topics—from the underlying Common Language Runtime (CLR) to its specialized packages for ASP.NET, Web Forms, Windows Forms, XML and data access (ADO.NET). The authors survey each of the major .NET languages, including Visual Basic .NET, C# and Managed C++.

Learning C#

By Jesse Liberty
1st Edition September 2002
368 pages, ISBN 0-596-00376-5

With *Learning C#*, best-selling author Jesse Liberty will help you build a solid foundation in .NET and show how to apply your skills by using dozens of tested examples. You will learn how to develop various kinds of applications—including those that work with databases—and web services. Whether you have a little object-oriented programming experience or you are new to programming altogether, *Learning C#* will set you firmly on your way.

COM and .NET Component Services

By Juval Löwy
1st Edition September 2001
384 pages, 0-596-00103-7

COM & .NET Component Services
provides both traditional COM programmers and new .NET component developers with the information
they need to begin developing applications that take full advantage of
COM+ services. This book focuses
on COM+ services, including support for transactions, queued components, events, concurrency
management, and security.

Object-Oriented Programming with Visual Basic .NET

By J.P. Hamilton
1st Edition September 2002
308 pages, ISBN 0-596-00146-0

Visual Basic .NET is a language that
facilitates object-oriented programming, but does not guarantee good
code. That's where *Object-Oriented
Programming with Visual Basic .NET*
comes in. It will show you how to
think about similarities in your
application logic and how to design
and create objects that maximize the
benefit and power of .NET. Packed
with examples that will guide you
through every step, *Object-Oriented
Programming with Visual Basic .NET*
is for those with some programming
experience.

Programming .NET Web Services

*By Alex Ferrara & Matthew
MacDonald*
1st Edition October 2002
414 pages, ISBN 0-596-00250-5

This comprehensive tutorial teaches
programmers the skills they need to
develop XML web services hosted on
the Microsoft .NET platform. *Programming .NET Web Services* also
shows you how to consume these
services on both Microsoft and non-
Windows clients, and how to weave
them into well-designed and scalable
applications. For those interested in
building industrial-strength web services, this book is full of practical
information and good old-fashioned
advice.

VB.NET Core Classes in a Nutshell

By Budi Kurniawan
1st Edition May 2002
576 pages, ISBN 0-596-00257-2

VB.NET Core Classes in a Nutshell,
provides a concise and thorough reference to the types found in the core
namespaces of the .NET Framework
Class Library. A companion to
VB.NET Language in a Nutshell, this
is a reference that VB.NET programmers will turn to repeatedly. Due to a
special partnership between O'Reilly
and Microsoft, this book also includes
a CD that integrates the book is reference into Visual Studio .NET.

O'REILLY®

To order: *800-998-9938* • *order@oreilly.com* • *www.oreilly.com*
Online editions of most O'Reilly titles are available by subscription at *safari.oreilly.com*
Also available at most retail and online bookstores.